Are We Missing Something?

How Scripture Can Guide Christians to Unity in the Twenty-first Century

Are We Missing Something?

Discovering God's House, God's Church, and True Worship

Keith Dorricott
Author of *I Want to Live*

iUniverse, Inc.
New York   Lincoln   Shanghai

Are We Missing Something?
Discovering God's House, God's Church, and True Worship

iUniverse books may be ordered through booksellers or by contacting:

iUniverse
2021 Pine Lake Road, Suite 100
Lincoln, NE 68512
www.iuniverse.com
1-800-Authors (1-800-288-4677)

Because of the dynamic nature of the Internet, any Web addresses or links contained in this book may have changed since publication and may no longer be valid.

The views expressed in this work are solely those of the author and do not necessarily reflect the views of the publisher, and the publisher hereby disclaims any responsibility for them.

First edition

ISBN: 978-0-595-43392-6 (pbk)
ISBN: 978-0-595-87718-8 (ebk)

Printed in the United States of America

Contents

Preface

Some Vital Questions

Is it possible for a Christian to be in the Body of Christ but not be in the house of God today? Is it possible for a church of Christians not to be a church of God? Is it possible for Christian worship to miss the mark?

The purpose of this book is to examine and explore three implicit beliefs that are very prevalent in the evangelical Christian world today. These are:

1 That the "**house of God**" refers to all those living believers who, by virtue of having the Holy Spirit dwelling in them, are in the Body of Christ. Therefore all believers have the privilege of spiritual worship to God as a priesthood, wherever and however it may be offered.

2 That every local gathering of born-again believers in Christ is a "**church of God**" (as the Bible uses that term). They gather on the basis of all being members of the church "the Body of Christ" (sometimes referred to as "the true church"). Which particular church group they should gather with is largely a matter of personal preference.

3 That the **worship** of believers involves the presence of God coming down to men and women on Earth wherever they gather for that purpose.

The three main sections of this book deal separately with these three issues. They also attempt to show how these issues are related to each other in one integrated pattern of scriptural teaching. The first section deals with the topic of the house of God—what it is, what it does, and who are in it. It traces the concept of God living among a people on the Earth, from the first reference in Genesis, through Israel's experience of it throughout most of the Old Testament, and then to its replacement by the spiritual house of today as set out in the New Testament narrative of the Acts of the Apostles and in the epistles. What becomes apparent is how pervasive a subject it is, and how central it should be in the life and service of disciples of the Lord Jesus today. It is not by any means an incidental topic. God will also have a house in the future, but this book does not deal with either the Millennial temple or the eternal state on the new Earth, which are both subsequent aspects of this comprehensive purpose of God.

Section two deals with the topic of the churches of God, as the scriptural gathering of disciples in this age. It addresses questions such as:

- Why are there so many Christian churches today?
- Can we be true Christians without belonging to a church?
- Does it matter which church we attend?
- Are we fulfilling the "great commission"?
- Is the apostles' teaching relevant in the twenty-first century?
- Is the New Testament just first century history, or is it also a blueprint for us?

The third section addresses the subject of worship. It asks whether all worship is acceptable to God and what true worship involves. It explores the particular character of collective worship and addresses the question "Where does true worship take place?" It also considers what impediments there are to worship that can detract from the pleasure that God wants to get from it.

Before proceeding with these key issues, however, there are two topics that should be looked at first, because they underpin what follows. Examining them beforehand will give a proper perspective on the issues themselves. These topics are:

- the special relationship that we as believers in Christ have been eternally brought into as members of "the church which is Christ's Body" (chapter 1); and
- a brief historical perspective of the development of the Christian faith throughout the centuries, which has led to our fragmented twenty-first century Christian world (chapter 2).

This book is offered to all true believers in the Lord Jesus Christ who are serious about their lives and service for Him, and who welcome opportunities to explore ways in which they may be able to please Him more.

In the pages that follow, as we delve into the highly relevant and inter-connected issues of God's house, God's church, and true worship, which are at the heart of the life and service expected of every disciple of the Lord Jesus, we shall have to keep in mind the cardinal principle that the Reformers used—"sola scriptura"—"by the Scriptures alone". The Scriptures, the written Word of God, will have to be the test of everything that we seek to discover. And then, as one Bible teacher put it, "If you show me what is in that book, you put me under an obligation to do it."

Introduction

1.

The Church that Christ is Building

"The church, which is His body, the fullness of Him who fills all in all."
(Ephesians 1:22,23)

When Christ told His apostles one day in Caesarea Philippi that *"upon this rock I will build My church"* (Matthew 16:18), He was announcing something totally new. Although it would be based on the eternal fact of His deity, as confessed by Peter, this church had not yet been brought into existence. The word "church" as used in the Bible does not have the same meaning as it is often given today, which is a physical building used for religious purposes. The word church in the New Testament is a translation of the Greek word *"ekklesia,"* from which we get our English word "ecclesiastical." It means people who have been called out to be together, a distinct assembly or congregation. Thus, when the Lord said that He would build His church, He was referring to people, and it was to be spiritual, not physical.

Old Testament clues

Various clues had been given about this church in the Old Testament, but never before had it been referred to explicitly. Later the apostle Paul would describe it as *"the mystery of Christ"* (Ephesians 3:4). What was this mystery and what were some of these pointers that had been given previously?

First of all, for instance, when God created the first man, Adam, He provided Eve as a wife for him (Genesis 2:21–25). However she was also a picture of this future company of believers who would become Christ's eternal companion, an illustration of the church the Body of Christ. Eve had been taken from Adam's side while he was in a deep sleep, just as this church is the result of Christ's deep ordeal at Calvary.

Another picture that is given is that of Asenath, who was the Gentile bride that Joseph had been given while he was in Egypt (Genesis 41:45). Joseph was heir to the promises that God had given to his great-grandfather Abraham. On the other hand, Asenath was a Gentile, an Egyptian woman, and so she did not have the same heritage. Yet she was given to Joseph to share his life and inheritance. Similarly the church the Body of Christ is not restricted to Jews, but is inclusive of all nationalities.

Although it had been hinted at back in Old Testament times, this church did not exist at that time. It did not apply to Israel as God's chosen people on Earth. It was something new that began when the present age began, after Christ's exaltation to heaven, on that day of Pentecost when the Holy Spirit was poured out (Acts 2:1–4). It required that the Gentiles be included so that it might be universal.

Building this church

The details of this church that Christ is building were revealed first to the apostles, including the apostle Paul who provided most of its teaching in Scripture, and through them to all the saints (Ephesians 3:2,5; Colossians 1:26). It was an all-inclusive message: all believers regardless of culture or background were equal members of this church, called "the church which is His body (Ephesians 1:22)." Each believer in Christ was then, and is now, built into it by being baptized by Christ in the Holy Spirit. Today this invisible spiritual baptism takes place simultaneously with the believer's new birth:

"By one Spirit were we all baptized into one body, whether Jews or Greeks, whether slaves or free; and were all made to drink of one Spirit" (1 Corinthians 12:13) [1].

Once believers are in this church, they cannot ever be put out of it or leave it. Their place in it is permanent. It is eternal and the Body itself is indestructible. Each believer is an indispensable member of it, like a part of a human body, and each member is intended to have an important part in its on-going strengthening (Ephesians 4:16).

We are told that Christ Himself cares for this church and preserves "her", because one day she will be united with Him as His bride (Revelation 19:7):

"Christ also loved the church and gave Himself up for her, so that He might sanctify her, having cleansed her by the washing of water with the word, that He might present to Himself the church in all her glory, having no spot or wrinkle or any such thing; but that she would be holy and blameless" (Ephesians 5:25-27).

This church began at Pentecost. Believers will continue to be added to it until the Lord returns to the air for her, at which time she will be complete and intact.

---

1   The original Greek shows that the baptism is "in" the Spirit. It is not the Holy Spirit who does the baptizing, but Christ Himself (John 1:33).

Those believers who have died will be raised; those still alive will be changed, and together—as one church—they will meet Him in the air (1 Thessalonians 4:16,17). And so the first time that Christ will meet His church bodily will be when He comes to the air for her. That is why the dead in Christ cannot go to meet Him ahead of those who are alive at His coming. He will meet her intact, as His bride—all believers together at once. That is what He is looking forward to.

The apostle Paul told the Ephesians that, when Christ returned to heaven, God His Father: *"put all things in subjection under His feet, and gave Him as head over all things to the church, which is His body, the fullness of Him who fills all in all"* (Ephesians 1:22,23). This tells us that this church, which would consist of all believers in Him from Pentecost on, is intended to be His "fullness," to magnify the glory of Christ, by being His complement. This will reach its culmination in the future, when all believers are perfectly united with Him and there is no created being outside His active authority.

Building up the Body

Meanwhile Christ continues to build up His church, by feeding her, caring for her, and holding her together, as believers hold fast to Him as Head:

> *"no one ever hated his own flesh, but nourishes and cherishes it, just as Christ also does the church"* (Ephesians 5:29);

> *"... holding fast to the head, from whom the entire body, being supplied and held together by the joints and ligaments, grows with a growth which is from God"* (Colossians 2:19).

He takes personal responsibility for her.

He does this through the work of the Holy Spirit, whom He has sent to indwell all believers, as He explained to His apostles on the night before Calvary:

- *"I will ask the Father, and He will give you another Helper, that He may be with you forever; that is the Spirit of truth ... He abides with you and will be in you."*

- *"The Helper, the Holy Spirit, whom the Father will send in My name, He will teach you all things, and bring to your remembrance all that I said to you."*

- *"The Spirit of truth who proceeds from the Father, He will testify about Me."*

- *"When He, the Spirit of truth, comes, He will guide you into all the truth; for He will not speak on His own initiative, but whatever He hears, He will*

speak; and He will disclose to you what is to come. He will glorify Me, for He will take of Mine and will disclose it to you."
(John 14:16,17,26; 15:26; 16:13,14)

Christ said that the believers who would come after Him would multiply the works of God that He had been doing in His life on Earth: *"I say to you, he who believes in Me, the works that I do, he will do also; and greater works than these he will do; because I go to My Father"* (John 14:12).

What should members of the Body aspire to?

It is the Lord's desire that the character and unity of this Body be reflected by all living members on Earth. For this to be accomplished, all these members must be fully linked together and be under the direct control of the Head, Christ Himself. Just as a human body cannot function properly if any part is missing, dislocated, or damaged, or if there is any blockage to the brain, so it is with the functioning of this spiritual Body. If there is any disunity or any disconnection from the Head, or any underdevelopment of any part, then the display on Earth of the nature of the relationship into which believers have been brought will be impaired. That is why Christ prayed to His Father on His last night:

"I do not ask on behalf of these alone, but for those also who believe in Me through their word; that they may all be one; even as You, Father, are in Me and I in You, that they also may be in Us, so that the world may believe that You sent Me" (John 17:20,21).

Not only would the behaviour of individual believers be impaired, but so would the fulfillment of the Lord's desire for believers to be together in unity.

Paul went on to tell the Ephesians what this building up of the Body was intended to result in. He expressed it this way:

"until we all attain to the unity of the faith, and of the knowledge of the Son of God, to a mature man, to the measure of the stature which belongs to the fullness of Christ" (Ephesians 4:13).

In other words, full maturity of believers together will mean that they express the divine unity which characterizes the church which is His Body.

This is not just describing the personal spiritual growth of each of us as individual Christians. It is describing the full coordinated development of such believers joined in divine testimony. He described it as the result of each individual member doing its proper part, being equipped spiritually to do so, and being fully joined together with the other parts:

"He gave some as apostles, and some as prophets, and some as evangelists, and some as pastors and teachers, for the equipping of the saints for the work of service, to the building up of the body of Christ … but speaking the truth in love, we are to grow up in all aspects into Him who is the head, even Christ, from whom the whole body, being fitted and held together by what every joint supplies, according to the proper working of each individual part, causes the growth of the body for the building up of itself in love" (Ephesians 4:11,12,15,16).

Paul said that we are to not be like children, but we are to become mature. (In 1 Corinthians 14:20 he elaborated on this by referring to being *"children in understanding."*) As long as we as believers together are lacking in our understanding and in our devoted adherence to all the teaching that Christ has given us to carry out (which is described as *"the faith"*), we will not experience our full relationship with Him. We will limit His work for us today as He lives and serves in the presence of God (the unity of *"the knowledge of the Son of God"*), to progress to this goal of expressing the full relationship implied in the figure of His Body. Paul warned the Colossians about the possibility of falling short of this when he wrote:

"Not holding fast to the head, from whom the entire body, being supplied and held together by the joints and ligaments, grows with a growth which is from God" (Colossians 2:19).

He was talking to them about indulging in worldly things or wrong teaching and practices. In verse 16 he had said, *"Don't let anyone judge you."* We are not to be influenced or led astray by any teaching, example, or criticism of others, no matter how convincing it may be. We are to keep pressing on towards the goal together.

It is about relationships

This imagery of a body is all about our relationships—with Christ as our Head, and with each other as members. The Body, with its different but inter-dependent parts, is all under the control of the Head. The supply of everything it needs in order to grow up and mature as one united person all comes from Him, but it flows to them through each other (Ephesians 4:15,16) [2].

But there is a lot more in the New Testament that applies to us as Christians than the teaching about the church which is Christ's Body, as wonderful as that is. When the apostles wanted to provide teaching on how disciples should gather

---

2   This interdependence is illustrated in Ephesians 5:22–33 by marriage between a man and a woman, which is the earliest and most intimate of all human relationships. The ideal in marriage is for the couple to achieve a relationship where each partner is so united with the other that they behave as one.

together, how they should serve God, and how they should deal with problems such as sin and disobedience, they did not use the imagery of the Body. Those are things that are dealt with in the teaching about churches of God and the kingdom of God, which are not identical to the church the Body, but are intended to depict it. For example, no person can ever be put away from the Body of Christ; his or her position in it is absolute, unlike their position in a local church of God, which can change. Also there is no reference to admonishing or disciplining other members of the Body, but there are such references to those in churches of God (Romans 15:14; 1 Thessalonians 5:14). The reason for this is that the church the Body is blameless and perfect (Ephesians 5:25-27), and this is what saints and assemblies on Earth should aspire to.

Fellowship within the Body

While all believers are members of the one Body and therefore do have an invisible spiritual connection with each other "in Christ" (Romans 12:5), in practice there can be limits to the fellowship they should have with each other. Paul shows that the Body can only function and be built up as it receives what it needs from Christ, and as it ministers those things to its members:

> "… and not holding fast to the head, from whom the entire body, being supplied and held together by the joints and ligaments, grows with a growth which is from God" (Colossians 2:19).

As a result, not all sharing that takes place among believers can automatically be assumed to be the fellowship of the Body. We are each responsible to hold fast to the Head by engaging only in teaching and service that is according to Christ and not to things that are of human origin (Colossians 2:20–23). This means that we each have to learn from Scripture to tell the difference. And so there can be limits in practice to the degree to which Christians may feel free to join in fellowship with others (1 Timothy 1:5).

Understanding this fundamental and unique teaching from Scripture about the church the Body of Christ is important for us as we begin this study of what the Scriptures teach about the three issues of God's house, God's church, and true worship. In this way we can properly relate it to, and distinguish it from, other things.

Why is it that this inherent spiritual unity among those who are "in Christ" in not evident today to a greater extent? Why are there so many divisions among Christians? For the answer to these questions, we will have to go back in history to understand how the Christian world developed to the state that it is in today. That is the subject of our next chapter.

2.

How We Got to Where We are Today

"I know that after my departure savage wolves will come in among you, not sparing the flock." (Acts 20:29)

The twenty-first century Christian world is very different from what it was in the first century. Unlike then, today there is a multitude of Christian churches, denominations, sects, and groupings. There is also a seemingly endless variety of "doctrines" and practices among them. These days a disciple of the Lord Jesus has to search for the truth of God. And it is not always obvious where to find it.

To understand how the present state of affairs came about, let us quickly trace the development of the Christian faith through the centuries, with particular attention on the teaching of the Lord to His apostles that was to be passed down.

The forty days

After His resurrection, the Lord Jesus spent forty days with His eleven apostles. He was preparing them to carry on His work after His departure. During that time, *"He had by the Holy Spirit given orders to the apostles whom He had chosen. To these He also presented Himself alive after His suffering, by many convincing proofs, appearing to them over a period of forty days and speaking of the things concerning the kingdom of God"* (Acts 1:2,3).

The culmination of that instruction was what is often referred to as the "Great Commission": *"Jesus came up and spoke to them, saying, 'All authority has been given to Me in heaven and on earth. Go therefore and make disciples of all the nations, baptizing them in the name of the Father and the Son and the Holy Spirit, teaching them to observe all that I commanded you; and lo, I am with you always, even to the end of the age'"* (Matthew 28:18–20).

We are not told the details of what He taught them during those forty days, but we can deduce it very clearly from what they did after He left, as recorded for us in the Acts of the Apostles and the epistles.

Pentecost

After the Lord had left His apostles and ascended to heaven, they and His other followers waited together in Jerusalem, as He had told them to. When the Day of Pentecost arrived, the Holy Spirit descended on them all, and Peter preached the first gospel sermon of the new era to those who came to investigate. The result was that about three thousand of them believed, were baptized, and were added together to those already there. And so there came into existence at the same time two vitally significant but different entities that would continue in parallel—the church the Body of Christ, consisting of all believers in Christ, having been baptized in the Holy Spirit (Acts 2:38) (which we looked at in the previous chapter), and the church of God in Jerusalem (see Acts 8:3 and Galatians 1:13), consisting of all baptized disciples who would continue consistently in what they were being taught.

What they were being taught became known as "the apostles' teaching" (or "apostles' doctrine," Acts 2:42). The apostles taught it, but what they taught were the commands that they had originally received from the Lord, which later became known as "the faith" (Acts 6:7).

This church in Jerusalem continued to grow, until persecution from the Jews forced most of them to leave the city. Other churches of God sprang up in the towns and cities where they went. These churches were all founded on the same teaching, and they stayed linked with each other. They were a community, which later was referred to as *"the fellowship of His Son, Jesus Christ our Lord"* (1 Corinthians 1:9 NKJV). This unity of teaching and fellowship was maintained initially by the apostles and other prophets, primarily by their visits (e.g. Acts 8:14; 11:22) and writings. But gradually other elders were appointed in the churches (first mentioned in Acts 11:30) to oversee them and to care for the saints in them. The New Testament records that by the end of the first century the work had spread throughout the eastern and northern Mediterranean areas of the Roman Empire, and it names many individual such churches of God.

The end of the apostolic period

By the end of the first century, all the apostles had died. They could not be replaced by others because a requirement to be an apostle of the Lord Jesus was that a man must have seen Him in resurrection and have been personally commissioned by Him. The foundation teaching that the apostles had laid down in every place was complete by this time. It was, as Jude described it, *"the faith which was once for all handed down to the saints"* (Jude verse 3). However, as the years went by, many of these fundamental teachings began to be lost, and the churches increasingly allowed error and human tradition to come in. This inevitably brought divisions among them. The apostle Paul had seen this coming. In his epistles to Timothy, he wrote,

- *"The Spirit explicitly says that in later times some will fall away from the faith"* (1 Timothy 4:1).

- *"The time will come when they will not endure sound doctrine; but wanting to have their ears tickled, they will accumulate for themselves teachers in accordance to their own desires, and will turn away their ears from the truth and will turn aside to myths."* (2 Timothy 4:3,4)

For example, the church in Ephesus to which Paul had previously written an epistle (Ephesians 1:1) was in danger of having its divine lamp stand removed (Revelation 2:5); that is, God would no longer have recognized it as one of His churches. In that epistle, Paul had been able to dwell at length on the marvellous truth of the church which is the Body of Christ (as we looked at in the last chapter), but by this time the saints needed to be warned that they had left their first love and needed to repent.

Deepening decline

The deterioration continued and the Scriptures became practically unavailable to most people, many of whom were illiterate, and they were eventually banned from public use in many places. Some of the developments that eroded the teaching of the Lord were as follows:

- By the second century, baptism came to be regarded as necessary for salvation. Later immersion was replaced by sprinkling, and then infants began to be sprinkled in the hope of ensuring their salvation.

- Around the same time, a trend was emerging whereby clergy were being appointed, distinct from the congregations, headed by a "president" (presiding bishop) in each church, taking over the leadership and all active service. The people were told that they could not serve God without these men as priests.

- As early as the second century, a variety of holy days and mandatory days of fasting was introduced and legislated.

- In the third century, the concept was introduced (later called "purgatory") of an intermediate destination of the souls of the dead. These souls, it was taught, could only be released to heaven by payment of money and by prayers to dead saints. This eventually led to the idolatrous worship of Mary the mother of Jesus.

- By the fourth century, the simple remembrance of the Lord Jesus in the bread and wine was replaced by a sacrificial "mass," in which the bread and wine were considered to be "trans-substantiated" into the actual body and blood of the Lord (although this term was not used until later).

- In the fourth century, the adoption of the Christian religion by the emperor Constantine brought about the union of church and state, and the doctrines of the church were formalized at the Council of Nicea. It declared, among other things, that eternal salvation was only available by keeping a number of "sacraments" (such as baptism, confirmation, the Eucharist, and penance).

- This was followed by a split between the Roman church in the west, and the orthodox churches in the east. In the Roman church, the Bible began to be withheld from everyone other than the clergy. It was generally only available in Latin, which very few people could read. Other books came to be regarded as of equal or greater authority, and the hierarchy of the church set itself up as the sole interpreter of the Bible.

- Subsequently, indulgences to atone for wrongdoing began to be sold (sometimes in advance) to raise funds for building basilicas and for other church purposes.

- In the sixth century, the position of pope ("father") was established as the leader of the Roman church. By the twelfth century popes were being established as heads of state, and in the nineteenth century the pope came to be considered as infallible.

Rediscovering the light

In the midst of all this darkness and error, it was the Protestant Reformation in Europe in the fourteenth to sixteenth centuries that largely began to reverse the decline. Beginning with godly men such as John Wycliffe, Martin Luther, and William Tyndale, the essential truth of salvation by the grace of God, by faith alone, was rediscovered. The Reformers' motto was *"sola scriptura"*—"by the Scriptures alone." They rejected the church's claim to be solely entitled to interpret Scripture and to modify its teaching in the light of experience. They studied the Scriptures for themselves. Wycliffe, Tyndale and others began making Bibles available. Wycliffe stated: "The knowledge of the revealed will of God is to be found alone in the Scriptures." The invention of the printing press by Johan Gutenberg in 1454 made possible more widespread distribution of Bibles and accelerated this process.

In the centuries that followed, more and more of the fundamentals of the apostles' original teaching were uncovered, as the Word of God became increasingly the subject of enlightened study by Christians. Valuable truths emerged, such as those pertaining to the church the Body of Christ, disciples' baptism, the Lord's Supper, and the importance of evangelism and good works. Gradually these truths began to be put into practice in place of the wrong teachings and practices that were so entrenched. It is always the case that, when the truth of God is discovered from the Word of God and is then applied, things begin to change.

It was in many ways similar to what had happened late in Israel's history, when the book of the law was found after it had been missing for many years. This was the book in which Moses had written the commandments of the Lord at Sinai centuries before. Hilkiah the priest found it in the house of the Lord, which was in disuse and disarray at that time, and it led to the reforms that King Josiah initiated:

> *"Then Hilkiah the high priest said ... 'I have found the book of the law in the house of the LORD.' And Hilkiah gave the book to Shaphan who read it ... And Shaphan read it in the presence of the king ... When the king heard the words of the book of the law, he tore his clothes ... The king went up to the house of the LORD and all the men of Judah and all the inhabitants of Jerusalem with him, and the priests and the prophets and all the people, both small and great; and he read in their hearing all the words of the book of the covenant which was found in the house of the LORD. The king stood by the pillar and made a covenant before the LORD, to walk after the LORD, and to keep His commandments and His testimonies and His statutes with all his heart and all his soul, to carry out the words of this covenant that were written in this book. And all the people entered into the covenant"* (2 Kings 22:8–11; 2 Kings 23:2,3).

However, as a general rule, as truth was rediscovered from the Bible it was not widely embraced. There tended to be resistance to any such change and new teaching. Just as today, it was hard to distinguish between what was true scriptural teaching and what was human tradition, and it was even harder to reach agreement and to institute changes as a result of new scriptural revelation. It therefore usually required those who held a conviction about such truth to break away from existing churches in order to put into practice what they had learned. Inevitably this process was slow and not at all peaceful.

That is why the Christian world today is so fragmented. That is why there is such a variety of denominations, with so many different versions of "the truth" and differing views on the relevance of certain aspects of the Lord's teaching.

Unfinished business

However, in all this marvellous recovery, some key aspects remained hidden to many Christians. These included God's continuing desire to have a collective people gathered on Earth that He could call His own and live among—an identifiable people who were living holy and obedient lives in unity with one another. This unity, not achieved by compromise, but by reaching a common and proper understanding of, and subjection to, the complete revealed truth of God, has been elusive over the years, and yet it is vital. To some Christians, the present diversity of belief and practice among believers appears not to give cause for concern. Rejoicing in the fact of us being *"all one in Christ Jesus"* (Galatians 3:28), as we do, they appear never to have seen what God intends for us beyond that. Surely if we miss that, we are missing much—and so is the Lord.

As we saw previously, on the last night of His life the Lord Jesus prayed for this unity of those who would believe on Him through what the apostles would teach:

> *"I do not ask on behalf of these alone, but for those also who believe in Me through their word; that they may all be one; even as You, Father, are in Me and I in You, that they also may be in Us, so that the world may believe that You sent Me. The glory which You have given Me I have given to them, that they may be one, just as We are one; I in them and You in Me, that they may be perfected in unity, so that the world may know that You sent Me, and loved them, even as You have loved Me"* (John 17:20–23).

His prayer, *"that they all may be one,"* was not a reference to their unity as members of the Body of Christ. That spiritual unity is guaranteed and cannot be lost. He did not need to pray for that. He was praying that believers would all be united in their service and lives for Him—that they might all truly be "one." And yet that certainly is not the case today. The unity of the Body of Christ is not seen in practice amongst believers today. Expressing that unity remains unfinished business of the highest priority.

The path to unity

What then is the key to achieving this unity that Christ prayed for? Is it for us to disregard our differences of views and just all get along with each other? No—surely it is much, much more than that. It is nothing less than having a united understanding and adherence to all that the Lord taught His apostles and that they then taught to others. It involves putting it into practice in an actual fellowship, *"the fellowship of God's Son"* (1 Corinthians 1:9 NKJV). This requires that we understand from Scripture all that He has commanded us, as the Great Commission states.

If this goal is to be achieved to any degree today, it has to begin with us having a proper and shared understanding of the Word of God, and how it applies to us today. Any accord has to be based firmly on what the Scriptures actually say and mean in order to be *"the unity of the Spirit"* (Ephesians 4:3). The Holy Spirit will not lead us into anything that is contrary to His Word. The Lord Jesus said that one of the reasons the Spirit would be given would be to lead us into the truth (John 16:13).

Discovering God's House

The House of God—Where God Desires to Live Among His People on Earth

"You also, as living stones, are being built up as a spiritual house" (1 Peter 2:5)

3.

Something More Than the Body

"One thing I have asked from the LORD, that I shall seek: that I may dwell in the house of the LORD all the days of my life, to behold the beauty of the LORD and to meditate in His temple." (Psalm 27:4)

When David wrote these words in Psalm 27 he was expressing his deep and chief desire to dwell where God dwells. He certainly was not talking about just going to church. He was talking about where he was most at home, where he wanted to spend his time, and with whom he wanted to spend it. As a man after God's own heart (1 Samuel 13:14) David wanted God's house to be the focal point of his life. Yet David did not have the opportunity to experience it the way that we can today, as disciples of the Lord Jesus Christ. It would take the future death, resurrection, and exaltation of Christ to make that possible. But we can only experience such dwelling by God with us if we first realize what the house of God is, and that it is in fact a possibility for us.

Why did David want so much to live where God lived? It was because he knew that this was where he would come to know God the best. He knew it would allow him to have the closest and most lasting relationship with the Lord. We see people at their fullest when we see them where they live. As David said in the previous Psalm, *"O LORD, I love the habitation of Your house and the place where Your glory dwells"* (Psalm 26:8).

What was it that David longed to see about God that we might miss? What is God really like in heaven? We are told that He lives in unapproachable light and brightness (1 Timothy 6:16), that there is total joy in His presence (Psalm 16:11), and that His will is always entirely carried out there (Matthew 6:10). Further, God's unlimited power and authority are seen as He directs the activities of the countless mighty angels that surround His throne, as they cover their faces and execute His every command (Psalm 103:20). From there, too, God's kindness and love are seen in His full provision for all His creatures (Acts 14:17), and above all in His salvation for mankind (which is only partly seen on Earth).

These (and more) are aspects of Almighty God that are also in view where He dwells on Earth. David knew that, while we can see glimpses of them from outside His house, in order to see them more fully we have to come inside. Nevertheless he knew that all the days of his earthly life he could only experience God in His dwelling place on Earth, which was but a copy and a shadow of the true tabernacle in the heavens (Hebrews 8:5; 9:23).

Where does God live today?

The concept of the eternal God living with people in a "house" on Earth may seem strange. Even Solomon posed the question, *"Will God indeed dwell with mankind on the earth? Behold, heaven and the highest heaven cannot contain You"* (2 Chronicles 6:18). The subject of God living in a "house" on Earth among a people of His own is not one we hear a lot about today. And yet it is a subject that runs from Genesis to Revelation. When someone refers these days to "the house of God," more often than not they are talking about a church or a synagogue or a temple of some sort—a building, a "place of worship" where people can go for religious activity. But that is not what the Bible means when it uses that expression. Happily there is much in Scripture which not only tells us of the reality of God dwelling on Earth, but also of how it is possible for us to be part of it.

Has God ever lived on Earth?

The Old Testament is full of references to God's house. It began with the dream that Jacob had at Bethel (with the famous "Jacob's ladder" that is sung about). It continued through the Israelites' construction of the tabernacle in the wilderness, then Solomon's great temple in Jerusalem and its partial restoration later under the leadership of Ezra. And then when Christ came to Earth about four centuries later, the temple, then rebuilt by Herod, was still the centre of Israel's religious life.

It continued that way, despite God having deserted it (Matthew 23:38; 27:51), until the temple was destroyed by the Romans in AD 70. But by that time the Christian era was in full swing. The disciples of Christ who gathered together in service did not have a central site, and church buildings were not a feature of their activity. In fact, they sometimes had to meet in secret because of persecution. Those early disciples often met in small groups in homes or in public places. It was only after the Roman Emperor Constantine converted to Christianity in the early fourth century that Christians began to build large, impressive cathedrals and other places of worship. But did any of these constitute God's house? Did God reside in those buildings? Was that where people had to go to be in His presence?

Is the church the Body the house of God?

Many believers today have some understanding of what the church the Body of Christ is. It is a uniquely New Testament truth. There often seems to be an assumption, however, that other things which are called "of God," such as "the kingdom of God," the "church of God," and the "house of God," are synonyms for the Body of Christ, and therefore everything that we are told about them automatically applies to all living believers.

However if, as we have been seeing, there is not presently a unity among believers alive today on the Earth, what is the basis on which we can all claim to be part of any of these other things? Can God live in a divided house? Does He have a divided kingdom? We need to explore whether there is in fact something missing in this explanation, that there is something additional that God wants us to put into practice today, something distinct from the wonderful reality of being members of the church which is Christ's Body.

Are our bodies the house of God?

When a person puts faith in Christ for salvation, we are told that the Holy Spirit of God takes up permanent residence in their body, making it a "temple" (1 Corinthians 6:19), a place where God resides. The Lord Jesus had promised His apostles on the night before His death that the Spirit of God, who to that point had been "with" them, would soon be "in" them (John 14:17). He was referring to what would begin on the day of Pentecost, when the Holy Spirit would be poured out on them, and they would be baptized in the Holy Spirit. This was going to be a very new and fundamentally different experience for them and for all believers.

The Lord had previously spoken about this when He was in Jerusalem at the feast of tabernacles. He had called out to those who were busily engaged in the temple grounds on the final day of the feast: *"If anyone is thirsty, let him come to me and drink. He who believes in Me, as the Scripture said, 'From his innermost being will flow rivers of living water.' But this He spoke of the Spirit, whom those who believed in Him were to receive; for the Spirit was not yet given, because Jesus was not yet glorified"* (John 7:37–39).

It would require the glorification of Christ in heaven after His resurrection to make possible this wonderful provision of the Spirit of God to permanently dwell in all those who would put their faith in Christ. As the apostle Paul later explained: *"Do you not know that your body is a temple of the Holy Spirit, who is in you, whom you have from God?"* (1 Corinthians 6:19)

The Spirit has been given to us in order to be a guarantee of our eternal salvation (Ephesians 1:13), to lead us as disciples in our transformation as sons of God into likeness to Christ (Romans 8:14), and also to be the power source of our service for Him (Acts 1:8).

Christ had referred to His own physical body as being a temple when He said to the Jews, *"Destroy this temple, and in three days I will raise it up"* (John 2:19). They had thought He was referring to Herod's great temple in Jerusalem, and they reacted strongly against His statement. They used it in their accusations against Him at His trial, misquoting Him in the process. But He was speaking about His own impending death and resurrection. He was talking about His own body being a temple, so making the first reference to the human body as a temple.

For every believer in Christ today the same thing is wonderfully true—that their body is a temple of the Holy Spirit; God Himself lives within them. But is that what puts them in God's house? Or is there something else?

Are we in God's house today?

What did the apostle Paul mean by *"You are a temple of God"* (1 Corinthians 3:16) and *"We are the temple of the living God"* (2 Corinthians 6:16)? What did the apostle Peter mean by saying *"you … are being built up as a spiritual house"*? (1 Peter 2:5) What did the writer of the epistle to the Hebrews mean by *"we have a great priest over the house of God"* (Hebrews 10:21) and *"whose house we are, if we hold fast …"* (Hebrews 3:6)?

Unlike the wonderful truth of the church the Body of Christ, this subject of the house of God is not something that is confined to the present Christian New Testament age, even though the house that exists today is different from what existed previously. It is a subject that begins right back in the book of Genesis and pervades most of Scripture. It was central to the experience of the people of Israel with God in the Old Testament, it continues for us in the present, and it will do so in the future. There are many lessons about it from Israel's past that can really help us to understand how it applies to us today, and so we will examine those next.

4.

God's House in the Past

"'What kind of house will you build for Me?' says the LORD, 'or what place is there for my repose? Was it not My hand that made all these things?'" (Acts 7:49,50)

While God has only had one house on Earth at any one time, throughout the centuries it has taken different forms in successive periods. Like so many other subjects in Scripture it begins in Genesis where Jacob's revelation plants many of the seeds of what would be revealed later. While he was on his journey from home, Jacob stopped at a place called Luz, just north of modern Jerusalem. While he slept he had a dream in which God showed Himself and confirmed to him the covenant that He had previously made with his grandfather Abraham and his father Isaac. In his dream, Jacob saw a ladder set up on the Earth that reached into heaven, with the Lord at the top. When he woke up he said, *"How awesome is this place! This is none other than the house of God, and this is the gate of heaven"* (Genesis 28:17).

And so he named the place Bethel, meaning "the house of God." There was no building or other sign of habitation there. But Jacob had learned that the key thing about God's house is not what man builds. Rather it is that God chooses a place to dwell in, and it is His presence in that unique spot on Earth that makes that place God's house. To mark it he set up as a pillar the stone that he had been sleeping on, and later he returned to live there. This was God's first indication that He had a dwelling place on Earth in which He was prepared to company with men.

The revelation of the house of God in Genesis has a second part, whereby God required Jacob and his household to dwell with Him at Bethel: *"God said to Jacob, 'Arise, go up to Bethel and live there, and make an altar there to God'"* (Genesis 35:1). An altar was to be built and from that time forward, in God's dealings with His chosen people, the altar was irrevocably associated with the house of God. Those that dwelt there, in God's house, correspondingly had to be purified and to change their habits. Jacob renamed it *"El-Beth-el,"* "the God of the house of God," because he saw God there, which is the whole point of God's house.

23

Previously God had been referred to as *"the God of Abraham, Isaac, and Jacob,"* the God of individuals, but this was something more.

The tabernacle in the wilderness

About five hundred years later, Jacob's descendents, the people of Israel, accepted God's covenant at Mount Sinai that established them as His people. They were to be uniquely His holy nation, distinct among all the peoples of the Earth, and to be a kingdom of priests (Exodus 19:6). Then God said to them through Moses, *"Let them construct a sanctuary for Me, that I may dwell among them"* (Exodus 25:8).

And so, on Mount Sinai, He gave Moses detailed instructions for the construction of a tent (or tabernacle, meaning a dwelling place) and all its furnishings. The God of heaven was going to live among them in a tent, just as they were living in tents. The tabernacle itself was made of ten identical linen curtains. They had to be joined in a certain way, so that it would be a single covering (Exodus 26:7). When it had been finished completely in accordance with the pattern Moses had been given, the visible glory of the Lord came down and filled it (Exodus 40:35). It then became the centre of the camp of Israel during their time in the wilderness, as well as afterwards when they crossed into the land of Canaan.

Later Moses, when he was thinking about the unique privilege of God living among them, exclaimed to the people, *"What great nation is there that has a god so near to it as is the LORD our God whenever we call on Him? Or what great nation is there that has statutes and judgements as righteous as this whole law which I am setting before you today?"* (Deuteronomy 4:7,8)

It is important to realize what had led to this honour being given to Israel. They had been chosen by God, redeemed from Egypt by the blood of Passover lambs, "baptized" in the Red Sea (1 Corinthians 10:2), and then brought to Sinai. There they pledged their obedience, saying, *"All that the Lord has spoken we will do"* (Exodus 19:8). On that basis they were given the covenant and given the privilege of contributing materials to the construction of God's house on Earth. They did the work, but it was God's design to the last detail. Once it was completed, God's presence filled it and its service could begin. To them and to no other nation had been given *"the service of God"* (Romans 9:4 NKJV).

This tabernacle was not a creative invention by Moses. It was patterned after and served as a picture of *"the true tabernacle"* that exists in heaven, *"which the Lord pitched, not man"* (Hebrews 8:2; see also Hebrews 9:24). It affected where the various tribes camped; it affected the arrangement in which they travelled; and it affected their daily and annual schedule of activities. It introduced a divine order into their lives, which had not existed before. Having God living among them made all the difference. The tabernacle was where they met with Him; it was their *"tent of meeting"* (Exodus 40:2).

Israel alone was the people of God on the Earth, even though they were insignificant in other peoples' eyes, as merely a nondescript nomadic collection of ex-slaves without a land of their own. However Balaam, a foreign prophet who was allowed to observe them in their divine order as they camped in the plains of Moab, described them as they truly were: *"Behold, a people who dwells apart, and will not be reckoned among the nations"* (Numbers 23:9).

Soon afterwards, in his great closing speech to the whole congregation of the people who would finally go into the land (but without him), Moses said:

> *"You are a holy people to the LORD your God; the LORD your God has chosen you to be a people for His own possession out of all the peoples who are on the face of the earth. The LORD did not set His love on you nor choose you because you were more in number than any of the peoples, for you were the fewest of all peoples, but because the LORD loved you and kept the oath which He swore to your forefathers, the LORD brought you out by a mighty hand and redeemed you from the house of slavery, from the hand of Pharaoh king of Egypt"* (Deuteronomy 7:6-8).

Also the people were instructed that, when they did enter the land, they were not to offer and worship in just any place that they chose. God had designated a place within that land where He was to be worshipped: *"Be careful that you do not offer your burnt offerings in every cultic place you see, but in the place which the LORD chooses"* (Deuteronomy 12:13,14).

And so Israel uniquely had been given the privilege of the service of God, which was centred on the house where God lived among them. What an honour they had, but it brought with it certain obligations: of living holy lives (Psalm 93:5), of obeying the law of God, and of carrying out the many ordinances of divine service (Hebrews 9:1). God was now living among them, which made them distinct from every other group or nation of people on the Earth at that time (Isaiah 43:1–7).

The centerpiece of the tabernacle was the Ark of the Covenant, in the most holy place. Above it dwelt the presence of God among His people. God called it His "strength" and His "glory" (Psalm 78:61). When Israel occupied their promised land of Canaan, the tabernacle stopped its journeying and was placed in Shiloh, just north of Bethel (Joshua 18:1). However under King Saul, the Ark was taken away into battle against the Philistines, where it was captured. Then God *"abandoned the dwelling place at Shiloh, the tent which He had pitched among men"* (Psalm 78:60). The ark did not return to Jerusalem until years later, when David became king of all twelve tribes. Meanwhile the tabernacle itself (without the Ark) moved about to Nob, to Gibeon, and finally to Jerusalem.

The temple of Solomon

Five hundred years after Sinai, when King David wanted to replace the tabernacle with a more permanent and suitable structure, a temple, he was told that he would not build it, but that his son Solomon would do so. And so David prepared and stockpiled supplies for it. Just as Moses had, he received the instructions for it from God Himself (1 Chronicles 28:19). The only item that was carried over from the tabernacle was the Ark of the Covenant.

After David's death, his son Solomon did build the house for God. God had appeared to David on the summit of Mount Zion, the mountain of the Lord, the same place where Abraham had previously taken Isaac to offer him. David offered a sacrifice there, and God answered it by fire from heaven. When David saw this he said, *"This is the house of the Lord"* (1 Chronicles 22:1). He knew that this was the location that God had chosen for His temple to be built (2 Chronicles 3:1).

It was a glorious temple. Once again, when it was finished, the glory of the Lord filled it and the people knew that God's presence was among them. Again it was the focal point of Israel as a nation. It was on the site that God Himself had designated in the holy city of Jerusalem, on Mount Zion, in the land of Israel's inheritance. Israel's full worship and service to God, their daily offerings and annual feasts, all centered on God's house, the temple. When it was finished, the Lord appeared to Solomon and said, *"I have chosen and consecrated this house that My name may be there forever, and My eyes and My heart will be there perpetually"* (2 Chronicles 7:16). God had put His name on His own house.

The psalms

The psalmists frequently expressed what it meant to them to have this privilege of God living among them:

- *"How blessed is the one whom You choose and bring near to You to dwell in Your courts. We will be satisfied with the goodness of Your house, your holy temple"* (Psalm 65:4, written by David).

- *"Zeal for Your house has consumed me"* (Psalm 69:9). This is the Scripture that the Lord's disciples recalled when they saw Him angrily driving out the moneychangers from the temple courts (John 2:17).

- *"How blessed are those who dwell in Your house! They are ever praising You"* (Psalm 84:4). This is a psalm of "ascents," sung as the people were going up to Jerusalem to the temple for the annual feasts.

- *"I was glad when they said to me, Let us go to the house of the LORD"* (Psalm 122:1). This psalm of David is also a psalm of ascents.

The second temple

Several generations after Solomon, however, the great temple was destroyed by the Babylonians. God allowed this to happen because of the nation's continued disobedience. Its divine service came to a halt. The people were deported into captivity in Babylon. They were deprived of their collective service in the house of God. However godly individuals could continue to live devoted lives in their alien environment, as we see with both Ezekiel and Daniel, who prophesied during this period of exile.

Finally, after seventy years, permission was given for the exiles to return to Jerusalem. Every one of them had a choice to make: would they go? Most of the people had been born in Babylon and life was comfortable there. Why uproot themselves and go to a land they did not know? There was only one valid reason to go—Jerusalem was the place of the Name. God's house was there, lying in ruins. Only a small remnant did go, just over forty thousand of them (Ezra 2), but they went with happy hearts: "*Then our mouth was filled with laughter, and our tongue with joyful shouting*" (Psalm 126:2). Ezra the scribe and Zerubbabel the governor led them. Willingly they began reconstruction of the altar and the temple, but opposition from their enemies put a halt to the work for several more years until, at the urging of the prophets Haggai and Zechariah, the work was resumed. As God told the people through Haggai: "*Go up to the mountains, bring wood and rebuild the temple, that I may be pleased with it and be glorified*" (Haggai 1:8). Finally the temple was completed and its divine service recommenced (Ezra 6:14-18).

The structure was far less impressive than Solomon's temple had been, and it would have been tempting to dismiss it as being insignificant. It was made of inferior materials, and it did not have God's visible glory hovering over it. But it was still the house of God, and God accepted the service that was offered there, even though it was offered by just a remnant of His chosen people. He said that He still took pleasure in it. It was the obedience of their hearts that He valued. To dwell again among a people who loved Him sufficiently to obey His Word was something very precious to God—and to them, "*the sons of Israel, the priests, the Levites and the rest of the exiles, celebrated the dedication of this house of God with joy*" (Ezra 6:16).

The third temple

Finally this second temple was itself replaced under King Herod, with a structure that took forty-six years to build (John 2:20). This was the building that was in Jerusalem at the time the Lord Jesus was born. When He came to Earth in His humanity, as expected He frequented the temple. It was His Father's house, the house of God, and it was the focal point of the life and service of Israel. And so He did. He was brought there firstly by His parents, at forty days of age, as the law required (Leviticus 12). At age twelve he came back with them for the Passover feast (Luke 2:42), but then stayed behind. When they found Him He told them that He had to be *"in My Father's house"* (Luke 2:49). Even as a young boy He knew that He should be there to learn, prior to Him beginning His public ministry.

At the age of about thirty, as He began His ministry, Jesus came back to the temple and found that it had become very commercialized. Travellers needing to buy animals for sacrifice were being taken advantage of. This infuriated Him and He drove out the moneychangers in his zeal for God's house (John 2:13–17).

Later, because the leaders of the Jewish nation in Jerusalem had rejected Him, He announced that "their" house was left to them desolate. It was no longer going to be God's house. God was no longer going to be living among His people Israel: *"Jerusalem, Jerusalem, who kills the prophets and stones those who are sent to her! How often I wanted to gather your children together, the way a hen gathers her chicks under her wings, and you were unwilling. Behold, your house is being left to you desolate! For I say to you, from now on you will not see Me until you say, 'Blessed is he who comes in the name of the Lord!'"* (Matthew 23:37-39) They had refused to let Him draw them to Himself, and so in their rejection of Him they lost the privilege of divine service. However, things were about to change.

God wants to be at rest

After God had created the heavens and the Earth in six days, He rested on the seventh day. In doing so He established the unit of time of one week, which has been a mainstay of the working life of men and women. God's purpose in creation was that He might enjoy His creatures and have fellowship with them, that He might be appreciated and worshipped by them. Then sin came in to make this impossible without the work of redemption. Christ had to take on humanity and give His life to redeem us back to God. But this work of redemption has been accomplished, and so God is now bringing to completion His great eternal purpose. His work of creation is complete, and Christ's work, which He came to do on Earth, is also complete.

And so now God wants to enjoy His rest—not a rest if relaxation or inactivity but the full enjoyment and fellowship with the people that He created and has redeemed. That is what God means when He talks about His "rest." God's house is where He wants to be at rest with them: *"'What kind of house will you build for me?' says the Lord, 'or what place is there for my repose?'"* (Acts 7:49)

When Israel was in the wilderness at Kadesh-Barnea on the verge of entering their promised land, they refused to go in. God was furious with them, because that was the place of His intended rest with them, and they were depriving Him of it: *"I was angry with this generation … as I swore in My wrath, 'They shall not enter My rest'"* (Hebrews 3:10,11). He waited for the next generation, and they went in instead. Even then it was not God's final rest; there was something more to come: *"If Joshua had given them rest, He would not have spoken of another day after that. So there remains a Sabbath rest for the people of God … let us be diligent to enter that rest, so that no one will fall, through following the same example of disobedience"* (Hebrews 4:8–12).

The same diligent obedience is required of us if we would enter God's rest today, a rest which (as we shall see) is still associated with the house of God.

Does God need a building?

None of the buildings that served as God's house throughout the Old Testament were His final place of rest. As Stephen said to the Jewish Council:

> *"The Most High does not dwell in houses made by human hands; as the prophet says: 'heaven is my throne, and earth is the footstool of my feet; what kind of house will you build for me? says the Lord, or what place is there for my repose? Was it not my hand which made all these things?'"* (Acts 7:48–50)

Clearly, all these structures, from the tabernacle to Herod's temple, were just temporary, just physical representations of the spiritual reality. God Himself lives in heaven in the tabernacle not made with hands (Hebrews 9:11), where no human eye of ours can see, *"The Lord is in His holy temple; the Lord's throne is in heaven"* (Psalm 11:4).

However, it has always been God's great purpose to bridge the gap between Earth and heaven. That was the significance of the ladder that Jacob saw. Jacob realized that God's house on Earth is also the gate of heaven, the means of accessing God where He is. It was for this reason that Jesus the Son of God came to this Earth in human form. It was not only so that we, poor sinful human beings, could have access to heaven one day through salvation, but also that the redeemed could access heaven collectively. This is not just in the future; it is for us today. Christ wanted to make it possible for us to serve His God and Father spiritually in God's immediate presence in heaven during our lifetimes. He wanted God's dwelling place to be not only in heaven or on Earth, but for the two to be linked.

It was for this purpose that the Holy Spirit was given. From the time of creation (Genesis 1:2) it has been the work of the Spirit to bring about on Earth what God the Father in heaven wishes to be done. And so the tabernacle and all the temples that followed it were just temporary, physical replicas; the true sanctuary in heaven is spiritual, for God is spirit (John 4:24). Those physical structures serve as a parable for the present time (Hebrews 9:9). God's house on Earth today is a spiritual house, and we will look at that next.

5.

The House of God Today

"You also, as living stones, are being built up as a spiritual house." (1 Peter 2:5)

Peter wrote his first epistle to encourage disciples who were living in several provinces of the Roman Empire, and through them to us now. Being part of a Jewish dispersion, as believers they were also "aliens" who were being persecuted for their beliefs. He wrote to them:

> *"You have been born again not of seed which is perishable but imperishable, that is, through the living and enduring word of God ... Therefore, putting aside all malice and all deceit and hypocrisy and envy and all slander, like newborn babies, long for the pure milk of the word, so that by it you may grow in respect to salvation, if you have tasted the kindness of the Lord ... And coming to Him as to a living stone which has been rejected by men, but is choice and precious in the sight of God, you also, as living stones, are being built up as a spiritual house for a holy priesthood, to offer up spiritual sacrifices acceptable to God through Jesus Christ"* (1 Peter 1:23–2:5).

Being born again

He reminded them that their salvation experience had involved them being "born again" into a new life, not produced by something that could perish or expire, but by the eternal Word of God. Possessing this eternal life, they could never lose it. It was guaranteed by the Holy Spirit (Ephesians 1:13) and was in God's hands, not theirs (John 10:28,29). Just as God's Word cannot be destroyed, neither can the life that it imparts. Therefore they were able to be certain that their salvation was permanent. At this point they also had the indwelling Holy Spirit and were members of the Body of Christ. Did this make their spiritual experience complete? Far from it—it was just beginning, as he proceeded to tell them.

31

Growing as a disciple

He then referred to their growth through continually taking in the Word of God as disciples. They were growing up in their salvation in the same way they had originally received it, by drinking in more and more of the pure milk of the Word of God, the way a newborn child does. Putting this Word into practice involved them putting away sinful behaviour that belonged to their old nature. They could not have done that without the Holy Spirit being within them. They were disciples, but where would this discipleship lead them?

Being built into God's house

He then described how they became part of the spiritual house that God was building. They must come to Christ as their Lord—not just coming to Him once in a single occurrence, as they had done at salvation. (The form of the word "coming" in the original shows that it is repetitive.) They must come in on-going response of obedience to His claims on them. They were being built up with others as a spiritual house. They were being brought into line with Christ as the corner stone. The purpose of that house was to be a holy priesthood, to engage in priestly service as a people entirely for God. And the nature of that holy priesthood service was their offering up of sacrifices which were spiritual in nature, not physical, which God would accept, as they were presented through Jesus Christ.

Living stones

Peter was showing them, and us, that the house of God is no longer a physical place, or a structure. It is made up of people, "living stones", stones made alive by the Word of God and ready to be built into place. Christ Himself is described here as a living stone, as an "alive man," and so are we as His disciples.

Christ had been rejected by the Jewish leaders when He was on the Earth. He did not fit into what they were building, and so they discarded Him the way a builder would discard a stone that was unsuitable. He Himself had quoted this Scripture from Psalm 118:22: *"Jesus said to them, 'Did you never read in the Scriptures, 'The stone which the builders rejected, this became the chief corner stone; this came about from the Lord, and it is marvelous in our eyes?'"* (Matthew 21:42)

But God had taken Him, that stone discarded on Earth, to be the supremely precious and uniquely chosen "stone," and had placed Him in heaven as the very foundation stone, the "corner stone," of that spiritual house that He was going to build. Peter further quoted Isaiah 28:16 from the Old Testament, *"Therefore thus says the Lord GOD, 'Behold, I am laying in Zion a stone, a tested stone, a costly corner-stone for the foundation, firmly placed. He who believes in it will not be disturbed.'"*

These Scriptures, dating from hundreds of years before Christ, show that God had revealed His plan well in advance. He had revealed that there would be a spiritual house, with its corner stone laid in heaven, in which people would engage in spiritual service to God, based on their on-going faithfulness to Jesus Christ as Lord. It was Jesus' death, resurrection, and ascension to heaven that made this great plan possible.

The New Testament Scriptures that deal with the house of God today refer to it in two general ways. They address it as being a place to live and also as a building structure. Let's look at both of these concepts.

The house as a place to live

To the church of God in Corinth, Paul wrote, *"Do you not know that you are a temple of God and that the Spirit of God dwells in you? If any man destroys the temple of God, God will destroy him, for the temple of God is holy, and that is what you are"* (1 Corinthians 3:16,17). He also wrote to them, *"We are the temple of the living God; just as God said, 'I will dwell in them and walk among them; and I will be their God, and they shall be my people. Therefore, come out from their midst and be separate, says the Lord and do not touch what is unclean; and I will welcome you'"* (2 Corinthians 6:16,17).

Here the apostle uses the term "temple," because a temple of God is a place where God dwells. Paul is showing the house as a place for God, not just to visit, but to stay—a "dwelling place" (habitation) for God on Earth among believers who are identified as His people. It is therefore a holy place. This necessarily requires that those people among whom God is staying live holy lives and be separate from ungodly things. God lives among them in the person of the Holy Spirit, who is the person of the godhead who makes the presence of God a reality on Earth in this age. This dwelling of the Holy Spirit is in addition to His indwelling of each believer's individual body, as Paul describes in 1 Corinthians 6:19. And so the temple itself is indwelt by the Spirit of God, as Paul also stated in his epistle to the Ephesians, *"In whom the whole building, being fitted together, is growing into a holy temple in the Lord, in whom you also are being built together into a dwelling of God in the Spirit"* (Ephesians 2:21,22).

In addition, the apostle wrote to Timothy about proper conduct in the house of God, *"I write so that you will know how one ought to conduct himself in the household of God, which is the church of the living God, the pillar and support of the truth"* (1 Timothy 3:15). The word for "household" in this verse is the same word as "house" used elsewhere, but it is translated as "household" in some English versions to emphasize the aspect of a people living with their God. Also in this verse the house is referred to as "the church of the living God"; it is the congregation of those who have been called out by the one true God to be together for Him. As such, as this Scripture shows, it has a testimony on the Earth to God's truth and to a standard of godly conduct.

We can see from these references that the house of God is where God, through His Spirit, desires to live among a people who are His own and who are living holy lives for Him.

The house as a building

The second way that the house of God is characterized in the epistles is as a structure. Unlike Old Testament times, it is not a physical structure; it is spiritual in character, made of living stones, people made alive spiritually. But the use of a building structure is a helpful metaphor for us.

As we saw earlier, Peter describes how the house is continually being built up:

"Coming to Him as to a living stone which has been rejected by men, but is choice and precious in the sight of God, you also, as living stones, are being built up as a spiritual house for a holy priesthood, to offer up spiritual sacrifices acceptable to God through Jesus Christ" (1 Peter 2:4,5).

It is as believers, desiring to grow up (mature) in their salvation, come to the Lord Jesus to be part of the house that God is building, and then continue to do so faithfully, that the house is built up and can function as a holy priesthood to God through Christ.

Paul spoke to the Ephesians about this same building activity:

"You are no longer strangers and aliens, but you are fellow citizens with the saints, and are of God's household, having been built on the foundation of the apostles and prophets, Christ Jesus Himself being the corner stone, in whom the whole building, being fitted together, is growing into a holy temple in the Lord, in whom you also are being built together into a dwelling of God in the Spirit" (Ephesians 2:19–22).

These saints in Ephesus had been brought into this position by being established on what they had been taught by the apostles and New Testament prophets, and they were being continually built together to be God's dwelling place.

Thirdly, Hebrews describes the house as what God is building today:

"Every house is built by someone, but the builder of all things is God. Now Moses was faithful in all His house as a servant, for a testimony of those things which were to be spoken later; but Christ was faithful as a Son over His

house—whose house we are, if we hold fast our confidence and the boast of our hope firm until the end" (Hebrews 3:4–6).

The house that God is building today belongs to Christ; He is not just a servant in it but the Son over it, with all authority.

What is the house?

The picture that emerges from all this is not one in which all believers individually, or even the whole Body of Christ, are necessarily in the spiritual house of God today. Rather, the house of God consists of those faithful believers who have come to the Lord to function as His house for this purpose, who are living holy lives, and who appreciate and faithfully engage unitedly in the holy priesthood service of the house, as we will explore in the following chapters.

Stones

This metaphor that Peter used of living stones is in contrast to the "dead" inanimate stones that were used in building Solomon's temple and the others that followed it. Stones used in building work have always had a particular significance in Scripture, again beginning with Jacob at Bethel. Jacob took the single stone that he had used as a pillow and set it up as a pillar, a landmark of testimony. While it may not have indicated anything extraordinary to other people, it did testify that one person had been there for whom it had had some significance. It also showed Jacob where to return to and settle down after his time away.

Years later, when Joshua led the people across the Jordan into their promised land, he took twelve stones out of the river and set them up in a pile on the riverbank. These stones represented the twelve tribes of Israel. Again this was a landmark, a collective testimony to Israel's experience in that place. It (and several others like it) was used as a memorial for future generations.

Large stones were used to build Solomon's great temple. They were cut out from a quarry under the city of Jerusalem. They were brought to the surface and shaped before being transported to the building site and placed in the wall of the temple: *"The house, while it was being built, was built of stone prepared at the quarry, and there was neither hammer nor axe nor any iron tool heard in the house while it was being built"* (1 Kings 6:7).

In addition to building stones, Scripture also refers in various places to "precious stones," such as were used to adorn the temple that Solomon built (2 Chronicles 3:6). These were dressed stones which were well-fitting and finished. Precious stones will also adorn the future city of Jerusalem (Revelation 21:19). The apostle Paul told the saints in the church of God in Corinth that he had laid the foundation teaching in that place, but they were each to build on it with their works of service, which would be evaluated one day. He likened those works to either gold, silver, and precious stones, or else to worthless wood, hay, and stubble, which would be burnt up in the fire (1 Corinthians 3:10–15).

The foundation teaching of Christ ("*the apostles' teaching*" Acts 2:42), has been entirely laid down for us and we ourselves are intended to be the stones making up the house. It is then up to each of those who are in the house to be building it up (edifying it) by authentic spiritual service. How they do that will determine whether they "adorn" the teaching so that it is attractive to others: "*Showing all good faith so that they will adorn the doctrine of God our Savior in every respect*" (Titus 2:10). Thus disciples themselves as living stones are intended to form the house, while their service in it can beautify it.

Christ both a stone and a rock

There is a difference between the "rock" that Christ referred to in connection with the church that is His Body and the "stone" that is the foundation of the spiritual house in heaven:

- "*Upon this rock I will build My church*" (Matthew 16:18).

- "*Behold, I lay in Zion a choice stone, a precious corner stone*" (1 Peter 2:6).

As in the Old Testament, so in the New Testament, different words are used for "rock" and "stone," and they have very different meanings. A stone is moveable; a rock is not. In fact, the only time they occur together is in the expression "*a stone of stumbling and a rock of offense*" (Isaiah 8:14; Romans 9:33; 1 Peter 2:8 NKJV), in which they both refer to Christ.

Christ Himself is spoken of symbolically as a stone in several places. He is the stone "*cut out without hands*" referred to in Daniel 2:34 that would strike and crush the image representing the four Gentile super-powers. He is also, as we have just seen, "*the stone which the builders rejected*" (1 Peter 2:7), referring to the refusal of the Jewish leaders to accept Him. He is described as the "*living stone ... a choice stone, a precious corner stone*" (1 Peter 2:4,6) that God has laid in heaven as the foundation of His spiritual house. The Jewish leaders were confounded by the fact that Jesus was God's choice to be the heir of His kingdom, as He spoke about in the parable of the landowner and the vine-dressers (Matthew 21:33–43). They could not accept that this one was the centrepiece of what God was building.

But this symbolism of Christ as a stone in His exaltation as a man in heaven is different imagery altogether from Him being referred to as the "rock." For example, David said in 2 Samuel 22:2: "*The LORD is my rock and my fortress and my deliverer.*" He was referring to God being eternal and unshakeable. Christ is explicitly referred to as the rock that followed the Israelites through the wilderness and provided water for them: *"They were drinking from a spiritual rock which followed them; and the rock was Christ"* (1 Corinthians 10:4). It was a symbol that reflected His deity.

The Jewish leaders were offended by the claim that Jesus was God's Son. They considered it to be "blasphemy." And that was the basis on which the Sanhedrin Council gave Him the death sentence (Matthew 26:63–65) and sent Him to Pilate to have it carried out.

When Peter confessed to Christ that He was *"the Christ, the Son of the living God"* (Matthew 16:16), he was confessing Christ's eternal and unchangeable deity. And Christ responded by saying, *"Upon this rock I will build My church; and the gates of Hades will not overpower it"* (verse 18). The rock of Christ's deity as God the Son is the basis for the church that is His Body. It is an eternal unshakeable truth, distinct from Him being placed after His resurrection and ascension as the *"chief corner stone"* of God's spiritual house. Christ's deity did not depend on His successful lifework, but His position in heaven today does. He always has been the "rock," but He has also become the "stone."

But how does this spiritual house actually work? How does it function as a "holy priesthood"? Who are the priests and why are priests needed for worshipping God? Finding answers to these questions is the next step in our journey.

6.

The High Priest of the House of God

"Since we have a great priest over the house of God ..." (Hebrews 10:21)

Because the house of God is being built up to serve as a holy priesthood (1 Peter 2:5) it needs a high priest. A high priest is of necessity a man (Hebrews 5:1), and he acts as an intermediary between God and His people. He represents God to them and them to God, and makes their service acceptable. Further, to be the high priest, the person must be qualified and appointed by God Himself. Israel had a succession of them, beginning with Aaron (Exodus 28:1) and continuing with his descendants. Who then is the high priest of this new spiritual house, and what does he do?

God's oath

Is there anything that is sufficiently important to cause God to swear an oath? Yes there is. When Christ ascended to heaven after He had completed His work on Earth, He was appointed to the post of high priest by God not only saying it (*"You are a priest forever according to the order of Melchizedek"* Hebrews 5:6) but also by Him swearing to it with an oath. His word and His oath are two things that are unchangeable (Hebrews 6:18). It was a permanent appointment. God's double assertion shows how important the appointment of the Lord Jesus as high priest is, since only He (who is both God and man) is ideally qualified.

A high priest under the old covenant could only serve during his lifetime, after which the responsibility passed on to his eldest son. In contrast, Christ has been established forever as high priest over God's house. There will never be another one. His position as high priest will never end, He cannot fail in it, and He will never be replaced. Even in the future temple in Christ's thousand-year reign on the Earth, and after that on the new eternal Earth, He will be the high priest of people's service to God. And so the privilege we have today of access to God and service through Christ is established forever.

Christ's service in the holy place

When Christ lived here as a man, He came to be a servant. He was "the servant of Jehovah" (Isaiah 42:1). He said, *"The Son of Man did not come to be served, but to serve, and to give His life a ransom for many"* (Mark 10:45). This earthly "ministry" to others uses the Greek word *"diakoneo"* in the original text, from which we get the word "deacon," referring to a person engaged in serving others. Christ was, literally, a deacon on Earth. He was sent from heaven as God's apostle to proclaim God to men so that He could then go back into heaven on their behalf (Hebrews 3:1).

Christ is now in heaven. Hebrews 9:24 tells us that Christ, after His completed sacrifice at Calvary, went into *"heaven itself,"* above all the created heavens, into the actual presence of God. He is there now. He has gone in as a man, as Jesus the mediator of the new and better covenant. He went in as our forerunner (Hebrews 6:20) so that we would follow Him in, and He continues there as a minister in that sanctuary on our behalf: *"Christ did not enter a holy place made with hands, a mere copy of the true one, but into heaven itself, now to appear in the presence of God for us"* (Hebrews 9:24).

In that place, He is *"a minister in the sanctuary"* (Hebrews 8:2). That "ministry" is the exalted ministry of divine service (Greek: *"leitourgos"*). It is a very different kind of service than His earthly ministry, but He is still serving. His ministry, when contrasted with the service of the Old Testament priests, is described as being *"more excellent"* (Hebrews 8:6). It is what makes possible the spiritual service of the holy priesthood, and what makes that service acceptable to God His Father, as 1 Peter 2:5 states. Coming in any other way would be unacceptable.

And so we as disciples today do not need a person on Earth to take us to God in worship. Christ has been exalted in heaven to do that for us. Thus Christ, who is both God and man, is the only way to God (John 14:6), both in salvation and in service.

Our role as priests

The priests in Israel carried out many services in connection with the house of God. They offered on the altar the animal sacrifices that people brought, and they maintained the lamp stand, the table, and the incense in the holy place. In addition, the high priest represented the people as a whole before God, such as on the Day of Atonement, when he alone could go into the most holy place to make atonement for them. Without the high priest, the other priests could not have functioned. So it is with us today as a priesthood—we need our high priest.

But He also needs us. Just as the high priest of Israel needed to receive offerings from the people in order to present them to God on their behalf, so does Christ today: *"For every high priest is appointed to offer both gifts and sacrifices; so it is necessary that this high priest also have something to offer"* (Hebrews 8:3). The house of God cannot function without worshippers who offer. Christ takes our offerings, perfects them, and offers them on our behalf to God. The role of the holy priesthood, then, is to bring spiritual sacrifices and offer them to God through Christ.

What is particular about priestly service?

Offering spiritual sacrifices as a holy priesthood has a number of distinctive characteristics, such as the following:

- The worship is directed to God the Father, and not to Christ or to the Holy Spirit. (*"He has made us to be a kingdom, priests to His God and Father"* Revelation 1:6). We will see in a later chapter what is particularly significant about addressing our worship to "His God and Father."

- Christ's part in this worship is not to receive it for Himself, but to offer it to God on our behalf as high priest, as a man mediating in the presence of God. His part is what makes it acceptable. (*"Through Him then, let us continually offer up a sacrifice of praise to God"* Hebrews 13:15; *"… a holy priesthood, to offer up spiritual sacrifices acceptable to God through Jesus Christ"* 1 Peter 2:5).

- The worship is offered by a collective people, not just an aggregation of individuals. They have a distinct identity as the people of God, the holy priesthood. Holy priesthood service is by a united people, who worship as one. Those whom Peter had described as a holy priesthood, he also described as follows: *"You are a chosen race, a royal priesthood, a holy nation, a people for God's own possession"* (1 Peter 2:9).

The apostle Paul also referred to this collective worship in writing to the church in Rome when he said to them, *"Be of the same mind with one another according to Christ Jesus, so that with one accord you may with one voice glorify the God and Father of our Lord Jesus Christ"* (Romans 15:5,6).

This service of the collective priesthood is in addition to and quite distinct from our personal communion with God the Father and with the Lord Jesus, which each believer can enjoy individually by the Holy Spirit: *"Our fellowship is with the Father, and with His Son Jesus Christ"* (1 John 1:3).

A kingdom of priests

Not only were these disciples to whom Peter was writing part of the *"holy priesthood"* (in other words, a people totally devoted to divine service in the worship of God), but they were also described as a *"royal priesthood"* (1 Peter 2:9). This expression is actually the same as was applied to Israel, at Mount Sinai, when they were receiving the covenant from God and were told that they would be a "kingdom of priests" (Exodus 19:6).

There is an integral connection between disciples who are the spiritual house of God today (1 Peter 2:5) and those who are God's kingdom today (verse 9). Peter applied the different terms to the same people. The kingdom of God refers to those who are united under God and the authority of the Lord Jesus, serving Him together according to His commandments. A great deal of what is written in the New Testament is about how the kingdom of God is to function. That was the subject matter of the Lord's instructions to His apostles during His last forty days with them (Acts 1:3). Just as Israel was God's kingdom on Earth in the past and had God's house among them, so God's house and His kingdom are linked today.

We may sometimes hear or read the expression "the priesthood of all believers"—meaning that all believers in Christ are priests. This is too inaccurate an expression. All believers, by virtue of the new birth, have a birth-right to priesthood, but all do not exercize that birthright. Serving as priests is a collective activity. It is the work of a priest*hood*. It is therefore necessary to become part of the priesthood in order to carry out that service (just as an athlete needs to become part of a team in order to engage in a team sport). We sometimes refer to people "going into the priesthood" as a chosen vocation, to receive training and ordination as priests in a church. But, as 1 Peter 2:5 and Revelation 1:6 show, becoming part of this holy and royal priesthood takes place when a disciple unites with other disciples as part of the kingdom and house of God.

A living stone that is not built into the spiritual house does not fulfill its intended purpose, just as a priest who is not operating as part of the priesthood is not fulfilling his purpose. However, when disciples today do become part of the spiritual house of God, and therefore part of the holy priesthood, how do they go about offering their spiritual sacrifices? To answer this question, we need to look next at the subject of worship in the house.

7.

The Worship of the House of God

"A spiritual house for a holy priesthood, to offer up spiritual sacrifices acceptable to God through Jesus Christ." (1 Peter 2:5)

Worship is the primary purpose of the house of God. As we have seen, there is a high priest in place to enable this to occur. But where does it take place? Perhaps we may assume that when we gather together here on Earth for worship, Christ comes down to join us where we are. We may base this, for example, on Matthew 18:20: *"For where two or three have gathered together in My name, I am there in their midst."* But as the context of that verse shows, this is not referring to worship at all, but to decision-making and judgment in the church. And so we have to look elsewhere for the answer to our question.

Christ is in heaven

We know that Christ has been exalted to the right hand of the throne of God, and has been told by His Father to remain there: *"Sit at My right hand until I make Your enemies a footstool for your feet"* (Hebrews 1:13). And so Christ does not leave heaven. In fact, as He promised, the next time He will do so will be to receive us to Himself and take us bodily back with Him to enjoy His presence for ever.

Christ went into heaven as a "forerunner" (Hebrews 6:20), to pave the way for us to go there in worship, and He is now there on our behalf: *"Christ did not enter a holy place made with hands, a mere copy of the true one, but into heaven itself, now to appear in the presence of God for us"* (Hebrews 9:24).

If Christ our high priest is in heaven and we are on Earth, how can we offer our spiritual sacrifices to God through Him? Christ does not have to come down here to receive them. It is the Holy Spirit, who is within us, that enables our worship of God in heaven: *"We ... worship in the Spirit of God"* (Philippians 3:3). This is distinct from the individual communion that He brings about (2 Corinthians 13:14).

The Holy Spirit has been sent to us on Earth for exactly this purpose, to effect the presence of Christ in His absence (John 14:16; 15:26; 16:14). That is why, for example, the church in Ephesus was told that they were "*a dwelling of God in the Spirit*" (Ephesians 2:22). It has always been the work of the Spirit to bring about on Earth what God is doing from heaven.

Because God is spirit and desires to be worshipped "*in spirit and truth*" (John 4:24), the Holy Spirit enables us in our spiritual faculties to offer our sacrifices to God in heaven itself. Christ does not come down to us when we worship; we draw near to Him in spirit. It is the Holy Spirit who makes it possible for those of us who are living on the Earth to worship God the Father who is in heaven. Ephesians 2:18 shows how each member of the trinity is involved in such activity: "*through Him* [that is, Christ Jesus] *we both have our access in one Spirit to the Father.*"

Not only is Christ in heaven now, He is in the heavenly sanctuary, serving as high priest. Thus, if Christ remains in heaven, and our worship is offered through Him, then it must take place there, not here on the Earth. As He has already gone there, so we also can now enter the holy place: "*Therefore, brethren, since we have confidence to enter the holy place by the blood of Jesus …*" (Hebrews 10:19).

Where do we come?

The men of Israel came for worship to the temple on Mount Zion in Jerusalem. Today we have: "*… come to Mount Zion and to the city of the living God, the heavenly Jerusalem, and to myriads of angels, to the general assembly and church of the firstborn who are enrolled in heaven, and to God, the Judge of all, and to the spirits of the righteous made perfect, and to Jesus, the mediator of a new covenant, and to the sprinkled blood, which speaks better than the blood of Abel*" (Hebrews 12:22–24).

After leaving Egypt, Israel had to travel for many years to reach the place where God wished them to worship Him. He brought them into the land of their inheritance (Canaan). Correspondingly we have come to a "better country," to heaven (Hebrews 11:16). Within that country, Israel came to the designated mountain of Zion; we have come to the mountain of God in heaven (the heavenly Mount Zion). Then on that mountain Israel came to the holy city of Jerusalem; we have come to the city of the living God, the heavenly Jerusalem. Finally, in that city Israel came to the temple, the house of God. But they could only enter its gates and come into its courts (Psalm 100:4); they were barred from the innermost sanctuary by the command of the Lord (Hebrews 9:8). But we have come to the holy place of the sanctuary of God's throne where God is, together with Jesus our mediator. God has called us into His own immediate presence in heaven, to worship Him in spirit and truth. The worship of the holy priesthood takes place in heaven, in the presence of God, where Christ has gone and is today. There is no higher place.

This is an amazing truth. Christ is now in the presence of God as a man, as mediator of the new covenant. That covenant is eternal and is based on His blood having been poured out in death at Calvary and sprinkled (figuratively), that is applied, in heaven (Hebrews 9:23; compare Leviticus 16:14). He is the "great priest" (Hebrews 10:19) over the house of God, and so those in that house are not only allowed to come in, but are summoned to come in by God Himself. It would be wrong for us to refuse that call, or to "shrink back," as Hebrews 10:39 tells us. As a result, we have the strong exhortation: *"Let us draw near"* (Hebrews 10:22).

The way in

So much of the teaching of the book of Hebrews uses contrasts between the old order of Israel's service with the service of God today. These include the covenant at Sinai, the law, the tabernacle service, and the priestly roles of Aaron and his sons. Even though the tabernacle was only a replica (a *"shadow"* Hebrews 8:5) of the true sanctuary in heaven where we are enabled to worship today, access to its most holy place was restricted, except for the high priest. He was required to go in alone on the annual Day of Atonement in the tenth month. Apart from that annual occasion, the most holy place was hidden to the outside observer: *"The Holy Spirit is signifying this, that the way into the holy place has not yet been disclosed while the outer tabernacle is still standing"* (Hebrews 9:8). The veil separated the holy place from the rest of the tabernacle or temple and kept it hidden. It was also the first covering of the Ark of the covenant and the mercy seat when they were carried in the wilderness; the people never saw them.

In contrast, the people of God today have access through the veil, which is the present living body of Jesus Christ: *"Therefore, brethren, since we have confidence to enter the holy place by the blood of Jesus, by a new and living way which He inaugurated for us through the veil, that is, His flesh"* (Hebrews 10:19,20). The fact that there is a perfect man in God's immediate presence who is there on our behalf, and who has cleansed all our sin by shedding His blood, is what permits us also to go in now in spirit.

So ... let us draw near

Chapters 10 and 12 of Hebrews are the summit of the epistle. They describe the thrilling privilege of the collective access that God's people have now into His actual sanctuary in heaven. The previous chapters led up to this. The writer knew that it was vital for these early disciples to realize that this privilege had been made available to them, so that they could take advantage of it *"in full assurance of faith"* (10:22). It is just as vital that we realize it.

This is why chapter 11 is inserted, to present that great catalogue of faithful ones, the *"cloud of witnesses"* from the past (Hebrews 12:1), to urge us to have full assurance of faith, to draw near together in full confidence, and not to hold back. None of them had the prospect that we now have, and yet they were so faithful to what they were given, even to the point of death in some cases. This chapter 11 is encouraging not just our personal lives of faith but especially, as the context shows, our *"full assurance of faith"* (Hebrews 10:22) in united divine service as the people of God. Faith on our part makes us grasp that our worship in the holy place in heaven is real even though we cannot see it physically.

The first part of chapter 12 also amplifies this experience. It describes God's disciplinary process with us as His sons, so that we might share in His holiness and so avoid the danger of us shrinking back, which we are warned about in Hebrews 10:26-39. Verse 18 then resumes the portrayal of the worship of God's house by describing where we have come and who are there. It describes the great congregation in heaven itself, including countless numbers of angels, believers who died in faith in Old Testament times, and members of the Body of Christ who have died. They are all focussed on God on His throne and on Jesus the mediator who has made it all possible. This is the company that we as the holy priesthood are with spiritually when we worship. This is worship in spirit and truth.

If this describes the tremendous privilege now offered to us as disciples of the Lord Jesus Christ, we need to determine who exactly can take advantage of it, and what conditions they must meet so that they can be sure that they are included. Who for example was Peter referring to when he said, *"You are being built up as a spiritual house?"* (1 Peter 2:5) Who was the book of Hebrews written to, urging them to *"draw near?"* (Hebrews 10:22) What is required of believers in order to have this privilege? For the answers to this question, we need to go back to the third chapter of this epistle to the Hebrews.

8.

The Big "If"

"Whose house we are, if we hold fast our confidence and the boast of our hope firm until the end." (Hebrews 3:6)

Aaron was the first high priest of Israel, but Moses was the one charged with building the tabernacle. It was he who received the precise instructions on Mount Sinai, and he was told that it was essential that it be built exactly as it was shown to him. Moses followed the directions precisely, and so he is described in the New Testament as a faithful servant: *"Moses was faithful in all His house as a servant, for a testimony of those things which were to be spoken later"* (Hebrews 3:5). Because the faithful Moses carefully followed the instructions, we have today an incomparable teaching tool to aid our service.

It is all about faithfulness

In Hebrews 3:1–6, however, it is Christ's faithfulness in God's house that is especially highlighted: *"Consider Jesus, the Apostle and High Priest of our confession; He was faithful to Him who appointed Him, as Moses also was in all His house. For He has been counted worthy of more glory than Moses, by just so much as the builder of the house has more honor than the house"* (Hebrews 3:1-3).

Although Christ serves in the heavenly sanctuary today, His position is vastly different from that of Moses. He is not a servant, but the Son over the house of God: *"Moses was faithful in all His house as a servant, for a testimony of those things which were to be spoken later; but Christ ... as a Son over His house"* (Hebrews 3:5,6).

There is a big difference in status between a son and a servant in a household. The firstborn son was the heir; he was treated as the future head of the household. He had permanent status and rank in the house, whereas the servant was required to follow orders and could be discharged at any time. The servant's word did not carry any authority unless he was expressly speaking on behalf of the master of the house or his son [3].

The exaltation of Christ by his Father in giving Him all authority in heaven and on Earth (Matthew 28:18) included making Him Son over His house. He is its chief corner stone. He is the one who is first, against whom all others are measured and lined up, which tells us of His pre-eminence and authority. Included in that authority is serving as its high priest: *"Since we have a great priest over the house of God ..."* (Hebrews 10:21). As typified by Melchizedek, He is both king and priest (Hebrews 6:20; 7:1; Genesis 14:18).

God is the builder of the spiritual house today and He does it through Christ (Hebrews 3:1-6). Since more honour is due to the builder than to what he builds, Christ is worthy of more honour than the living stones who make up the house.

The condition

In addition to Moses and the Lord Jesus, Hebrews 3:1-6 refers to a third class of persons, today's disciples, who must show the same characteristic of faithfulness. The passage introduces a condition when it says, *"if we hold fast ..."* [4] This condition of faithfulness is that *"we hold fast our confidence and the boast of our hope firm until the end."*

This holding fast has nothing to do with us maintaining our salvation; that is totally out of our hands (John 10:28). Our hope in Christ for eternity is secure, and we have been given the Holy Spirit as its guarantee (2 Corinthians 5:5; Ephesians 1:13). Nor does it imply that those to whom the epistle was written were just nominal Christians who needed to become true believers. Instead this holding fast is about disciples of the Lord Jesus continuing to believe in this "hope."

What is our "hope"?

We tend to think of a hope as being something uncertain in the future, something that we are wishing for and looking forward to. And so when Hebrews 3:6 talks about us holding fast to our confidence and glorying in that hope, we might assume that it is referring to the future hope that Christians have of Christ coming from heaven for them. That is the hope that is referred to, for example, in Titus 2:13: *"Looking for the blessed hope and the appearing of the glory of our great God and Savior, Christ Jesus"*. If that were what it was referring to, then a believer

---

3   We get an illustration of this in the Lord's story of the prodigal son in Luke chapter 15. After the son returned home, he was willing to become just a servant in the house. He knew the difference.

4   In the Greek text the word for "if" makes it clear that it is a condition—"if indeed."

could belong to God's house only as long as he or she believed and looked forward to Christ's return.

But a hope can also be something we want now (such as, "I hope I am making myself clear in this book"). Hebrews 3:6 is referring to such a present hope, not one that we have to wait for, as these verses explain:

- *"This hope we have as an anchor of the soul, a hope both sure and steadfast and one which enters within the veil, where Jesus has entered as a forerunner for us"* (Hebrews 6:19,20).

- *"… bringing in of a better hope, through which we draw near to God"* (Hebrews 7:19).

This hope is the reality of Christ in the presence of God as priest on behalf of God's people, permitting them to draw near. Both of these verses are in the present tense; the entering and drawing near is now. It is a *"better hope"* than Israel ever enjoyed under the law. We are to *"take hold"* of this hope (Hebrews 6:18), and then to *"hold fast"* our confession of it (Hebrews 10:23).

In the Bible the word "hope" does not imply any uncertainty or something we may just wish for. Rather it is something invisible that we are longing for, whether in the future or now. What gives us assurance about its fulfilment is our faith: *"Faith is the assurance of things hoped for, the conviction of things not seen"* (Hebrews 11:1). Both hope and faith are stated in Hebrews chapter 10 as being critical elements in our spiritual access to God in worship: *"Let us draw near with a sincere heart in full assurance of faith"* (Hebrews 10:22); and *"Let us hold fast the confession of our hope without wavering"* (Hebrews 10:23). We have been given the hope; by faith we need to avail ourselves of it.

What is our confession?

Our worship to God involves us making confession [5] to His name. We are able to do this because we hold fast the confession of our hope, we believe and acknowledge the truth of God that has been given to us through Christ. Christ is referred to as the apostle and high priest of our confession: *"Consider Jesus, the Apostle and High Priest of our confession"* (Hebrews 3:1). As its apostle He was sent out by God to bring God's Word to us; as its high priest He has gone back in to God to serve as high priest on behalf of the people of God, who hold and keep that Word. By holding fast by faith to this confession, we are enabled to draw near into the presence of God.

---

5   The Greek word is *homologeo*, meaning what we acknowledge and profess.

One of the results of this is that we can draw near in spirit to God's throne to express ourselves to Him in prayer:

"... we have a great high priest who has passed through the heavens, Jesus the Son of God, let us hold fast our confession ... therefore let us draw near with confidence to the throne of grace ..." (Hebrews 4:14,16).

Another is that we can draw near in worship, by entering into the holy place (Hebrews 10:19-25). This involves us offering a sacrifice of praise pertaining to this confession:

"Through Jesus, therefore, let us continually offer to God a sacrifice of praise—the fruit of lips that confess his name" (Hebrews 13:15 NIV) [6].

What does it all mean?

Our participation in the house of God is therefore a conditional matter. It is conditional on our faithfulness in holding fast to our confidence in and glorying of our hope, whereby we continually draw near with a sincere heart as the people of God to worship Him together in spirit and truth through Jesus Christ our high priest, confessing God's name (and worth) to Him. As we hold fast we are able to continue in the house. If we willfully disregard it or neglect it, our place in the house will be in jeopardy.

The "pillar and support of the truth"

Paul is another writer who mentioned the conditions of being the house of God. When he was giving instructions to the young man Timothy about elders and deacons in churches of God, he described the house as "the pillar and support of the truth":

"I write so that you will know how one ought to conduct himself in the household [7] of God, which is the church of the living God, the pillar and support of the truth" (1 Timothy 3:15).

Paul's description of the house of God as *"the pillar and support of the truth"* means that it must stand for and remain faithful to the truth of God. Otherwise,

---

6   The Greek words for *"confess His name"* (NIV) are sometimes translated as *"give/giving thanks to His name"* (NASB, NKJV) and sometimes as *"make confession to His name"* (American Standard Version, English Revised Version).

7   The Greek word used here is *'oikos'*, translated "household" in NASB and NIV and translated "house" in NKJV and King James Version. It is referring to the house of God.

those in it cannot continue to be God's house. The condition of holding fast the confession of our hope, that we have just been considering, is therefore an aspect of a more comprehensive condition of holding fast to the truth of God.

This means that if error or division comes in among the people of God with respect to the Lord's teaching, their position as God's house is at risk. This is exactly what happened after the first century, when the apostles had passed on. Waves of wrong teaching came into the churches, as we looked at in chapter 2. God's truth was no longer being testified to and upheld. Exactly when God stopped recognizing them as His house we do not know, but it was not the first time it had happened. God had vacated His house before, as Christ had announced when He was in Jerusalem (Matthew 23:38).

What is "the truth"?

What then is "the truth" that is being referred to in 1 Timothy 3:15 that must be upheld? In the previous chapter, Paul had told Timothy that God *"desires all men to be saved and to come to the knowledge of the truth"* (1 Timothy 2:4). In his second epistle to Timothy, he referred to people who were *"always learning and never able to come to the knowledge of the truth"* (2 Timothy 3:7). And so this topic of "the truth" was a recurring theme of Paul's to Timothy. It referred to the whole body of teaching for disciples in that day (and today), and is also referred to also as "the faith" (see Appendix B). It is the whole gospel and counsel of God that apply to men and women today (Acts 20:27). It includes not only how to be eternally saved, but also how believers are to live, and how they are to worship and serve God. It is comprehensive.

When Paul said that the house of God must be its "pillar and support," he was saying that it must be a place of obedience to all the teaching of the Lord. Since the house of God is where God Himself lives and is served, it must also be a place of godly conduct and proper order. Doctrine (teaching) and related practice is thus an essential element of being the house of God today. Yet what we see today in the Christian world is a huge diversity of doctrine and practice.

9.

Growing into a Holy Temple

"In whom the whole building, being fitted together, is growing into a holy temple in the Lord ... "
(Ephesians 2:21)

The many Gentile saints in the church at Ephesus in Asia Minor did not have the same background as their Jewish counterparts. They did not have the same knowledge of the Old Testament nor the heritage of divine service from their ancestors. Most had been pagans, and the service of God was new to them. So the apostle Paul, whose special mission was to these Gentiles, assured them that they had been given all the same privileges as their Jewish Christian colleagues.

Full rights and privileges

In the second chapter of Ephesians, he reviewed for them their spiritual experience to that point. He reminded them of the state that they had been in before they came to Christ: *"dead in your trespasses and sins"* (verse 1) ... *"having no hope and without God in the world"* (verse 12). But then everything had changed: *"by grace you have been saved through faith* (verse 8). He said *"remember that you were at that time separate from Christ, excluded from the commonwealth of Israel, and strangers to the covenants of promise"* (verse 12). But now they no longer had an inferior status:

> *"So then you are no longer strangers and aliens, but you are fellow citizens with the saints, and are of God's household, having been built on the foundation of the apostles and prophets, Christ Jesus Himself being the corner stone, in whom the whole building, being fitted together, is growing into a holy temple in the Lord, in whom you also are being built together into a dwelling of God in the Spirit"* (verses 19-22).

Laying the foundation

Paul describes in these verses the structure and formation of that spiritual house that they were part of, the same house that we have been looking at, as referred to in 1 Timothy 3:15 and 1 Peter 2:5, and the epistle to the Hebrews. God has only one spiritual house for believers today. The apostle outlined that it began with Christ Jesus being laid by God His Father as the corner stone in heaven after His ascension, as 1 Peter 2:6 also describes. Then, corresponding to that foundation, the apostles together with New Testament prophets laid the foundation teaching as they established churches of disciples in various places in their travels. That consistent teaching was what the Lord Jesus had commanded the eleven before his ascension when He spent the forty days with them *"speaking of the things concerning the kingdom of God"* (Acts 1:3), and additionally revealed to Paul (Galatians 1:12–17; 1 Corinthians 11:23).

Each church (collection of saints) that was established on this foundation teaching in each locality was what God was building in that place. Paul used the same language when he referred to the church in Corinth as *"God's building"* (1 Corinthians 3:9) [8].

How many buildings?

Ephesians 2:21 in our English Bible translations can be confusing. This verse is often translated *"in whom the whole building, being fitted together, is growing into a holy temple in the Lord."* The word for "whole" is the Greek word *"pas,"* which is used frequently in the New Testament. When it is used without the article, as here, it means "every", not "the whole". Rather than this verse being translated *"the whole building,"* it is better read as *"every building"* (or as some versions have it *"each several building"*). [9]

Thus Ephesians 2:21,22 may be read (and interpreted) as: *"in whom every building* [that is, each local church], *being fitted* [joined] *together, is growing into* [the]

---

8   Paul did not include himself by saying "we," as he did earlier in that verse when referring to working with them for God, because he was not in the church in Corinth that he was writing to. Each church was described spiritually as a building. Together they formed the temple of God.

9   To illustrate this meaning of the Greek word *"pas,"* consider two other examples where it is used: (1) 1 Corinthians 11:3: *"Christ is the head of every man"*; this clearly does not mean *"the head of the whole man"*; and (2) Ephesians 5:20 *"always giving thanks for all things..."*; clearly again this does not mean *"giving thanks for the whole thing."*

holy temple [God's house] *in the Lord, in whom you also* [the church in Ephesus] *are being built together into a dwelling of God in the Spirit."* [10]

What Paul is describing here is each local church being established on the same foundation teaching of the apostles (and New Testament prophets), and being united to all other such churches, resulting in them all growing as the temple (house) of God on Earth. He then particularized it to the church in Ephesus, telling them that they also were part of it. They were a habitation [11] of God in the Spirit. In other words, God was living among them collectively in the person of the Holy Spirit; they were part of the total house.

This picture of many individual buildings (local churches) constituting one house is similar to the composition of the temple that existed in the Lord's time: *"Jesus came out from the temple and was going away when His disciples came up to point out the temple buildings to Him. And He said to them, 'Do you not see all these things? Truly I say to you, not one stone here will be left upon another, which will not be torn down'"* (Matthew 24:1,2). That temple had multiple buildings also. Peter does not mention the individual constituent buildings in his description of the living stones in 1 Peter 2:5; he was not writing to an individual church in that case, but to saints in various areas.

How the house is built up

In summary then, we can see that:

- Christ in His exaltation has been placed by God in heaven as the chief corner stone of the spiritual house (1 Peter 2:6).
- Churches of disciples (who are referred to as "saints," Ephesians 1:1) are formed on Earth corresponding to that foundation in heaven, by adherence to the uniform teaching of the apostles.
- Individuals come to Christ for salvation, continue as obedient disciples, and come to be added together as living stones, being built into this house (1 Peter 2:5).
- The individual churches are united in teaching and practice with each other; this outcome of *"the unity of the faith"* is the goal set out for all members of the Body of Christ (Ephesians 4:13).

---

10 One reason why this distinction between singular and plural is important here is that it can help us to avoid assuming that *"the whole building"* is referring to the Body of Christ.

11 Literally it means "a settled dwelling place"—Greek: *kat-oikeo*.

- Those churches together constitute the house (temple) of God on Earth, as God's dwelling place among His people (2 Corinthians 6:16).

- This house has the supreme privilege of united access into the presence of God in spirit, for the purpose of collectively offering spiritual service as a holy priesthood, through the ministry of Christ as high priest (Hebrews 10:19–23).

- If error is introduced and allowed to continue, or if those in the house fail to continue to give effect to their privilege of access in worship, they can no longer continue to be God's house (Hebrews 3:6). They cannot of course lose their eternal salvation in Christ, and they do not cease to be members of the Body of Christ.

This view of things is very different from what we get by assuming that all believers, by virtue solely of their membership in the Body of Christ, are in the house of God and have the privilege of collective worship as God's people. That assumption leaves out the essential requirements of adherence to the Lord's teaching, faithfulness in divine service, and unity. However the view that all members of the Body of Christ should be united in this way and have this privilege is very much the ideal that we should be striving for.

10.

Linking Heaven and Earth

"Behold, a ladder was set on the earth with its top reaching to heaven."
(Genesis 28:12)

The house of God in Old Testament times was strictly earthly, though it was a *"shadow of the heavenly things"* (Hebrews 8:5). The spiritual house of God today has both heavenly and earthly aspects. The living stones, believers, that are joined to make up the house are on Earth. They are disciples gathered together in accordance with what the apostles taught, and they enjoy its privilege of divine service. Their audible expression of worship uses their physical voices. But their access is into heaven itself in spirit, where God is and where Jesus the Son of God continuously ministers as their high priest. It is spiritual service.

This link between heaven and Earth is an essential element of the house of God. It is what Jacob was shown in the dream that he saw, as he realized that the house of God, where he was, was the gate of heaven (Genesis 28:17).

Lamp stands on Earth and the sanctuary in heaven

The tabernacle that Israel constructed in the wilderness had two compartments: a "holy place" and a "most holy place." Inside the holy place was the golden lamp stand, the table of showbread and the golden altar of incense. In the most holy place was the Ark of the Covenant covered by the mercy seat, above which dwelt the immediate presence of God. Today there is no division into two sections. These items of furniture mostly speak of Christ who is in heaven; however the lamp stand particularly speaks of testimony by saints on Earth today in local churches of God (Revelation 1:12).

Foundations in heaven and on Earth

God has placed Christ as the foundation stone of the spiritual house in the heavenly Mount Zion (1 Peter 2:6). Corresponding to this, the apostles laid on Earth the foundation teaching that they had received from Him, as they established churches in various places. If they had taught anything other than that in any place, the disciples in that place could not have been part of the house. Everywhere the apostles travelled, they established the same teaching, based directly on what the Lord Jesus had personally taught them. Even though the apostle Paul was not with the other apostles before the Lord's ascension, he also received the self-same teaching directly from the Lord (1 Corinthians 11:23; 15:8).

> *"According to the grace of God which was given to me, like a wise master builder I laid a foundation ... no man can lay a foundation other than the one which is laid, which is Jesus Christ"* (1 Corinthians 3:10,11).

This matching of the foundation teaching on Earth with what God had done in heaven is a fulfillment of the Lord's words when he taught His disciples to pray: *"Your kingdom come; your will be done on earth as it is in heaven"* (Matthew 6:10). What takes place on Earth must correspond to what is true in heaven, for God to live among us.

Service by a collective people

It is important to note in all this that the service of the people of God was and is primarily collective. The individual's contribution is always vital, but God always desires unity. Unity is at the very essence of the person of God, three in one, joined in perfect harmony and love. It is the unity that is reflected in the single name into which disciples are baptized: *"the name of the Father and the Son and the Holy Spirit"* (Matthew 28:19). For example, God desires unity when He joins a man and a woman in marriage. Again this is a three-way unity of the two people with Himself, which is why today marriage by disciples should be *"in the Lord"* (1 Corinthians 7:39). He wants this same unity in the people that He calls out to serve Him.

For example, Israel was covenanted to be one holy nation for God. They were to be united both with Him and with each other in the two greatest commandments of their law: *"You shall love the Lord your God with all your heart, and with all your soul, and with all your mind ..."*; and *"You shall love your neighbour as yourself"* (Matthew 22:37,39).

Similarly, when Moses was instructed to ratify the covenant that established Israel as God's unique people, His peculiar treasure (Exodus 19:6), he took blood and sprinkled both the book of the law and the people (Exodus 24:6-8; Hebrews 9:19,20). They thereby became jointly bound to Him by that covenant.

Although individuals in Israel brought offerings and engaged in certain activity, the focus was on the nation as one people—the particular individuals comprising it were secondary. For example, God had decreed that His people Israel would enter the promised land; that could not be denied. Yet certain persons failed to enter, due to their disobedience and lack of faith (Jude verse 5). But others took their place, and so God's promise was fulfilled collectively. They went in as a nation under Joshua's leadership.

In a similar way, the focus of the book of Hebrews is on the people of God and the privileges given to them. In it several specific warnings are given, including some to individuals which show that it is possible for any one person to miss out on the privileges that are made available to the people as a whole. For example:

- *"Take care, brethren, that there not be in any one of you an evil, unbelieving heart that falls away from the living God"* (3:12).

- *"Therefore let us be diligent to enter that rest, so that no one will fall, through following the same example of disobedience"* (4:11).

What God is looking for then is a united people who function together, with a single identity as one holy nation, one spiritual house, one priesthood. It is not merely an aggregation of individuals being in one place worshipping God, but a people drawing near as one. It is only by the work of the Spirit of God that this unity can be achieved in practice (Ephesians 4:3).

The Amen

This collective view of things helps us to understand the significance of saying *"the Amen"* (1 Corinthians 14:16) at the collective giving of thanks and prayer. When a church gathers to engage in this activity, several men may speak in turn, voicing the thanksgivings and prayers (1 Timothy 2:8). When they do this, they are not just speaking for themselves, but are representing the whole company. This is then acknowledged by all the others saying "Amen," meaning "so be it," and so associating themselves with what has been said.

Understanding this collective identity and functioning is a vital part of realizing the opportunity that is presented to us to be the people of God and the house of God today. How we gather on Earth in our service for God must reflect this unity and collective identity. How the Bible tells us that we are to gather in order to do this is the subject of our next section: Discovering God's Church.

11.

God's House—A Summary

The main points about God's house that have emerged in this section can be summarized as follows:

- God began to disclose His desire to live among His people on Earth in the book of Genesis.

- God's first house built by men on Earth was the tabernacle in the wilderness, given to His people Israel. It represented the true holy place in heaven.

- Today God's house is not only the result of the fact that the Holy Spirit indwells individual believers. It is God the Spirit living among a united people.

- The house today is spiritual. It consists of disciples being built together, on the foundational teaching of the apostles, to form local churches, which are united in that teaching and practice to constitute God's house.

- God's house is different from the Body of Christ in many ways, but principally because it requires on-going faithfulness to the truth of God to be in it.

- The house of God consists of people and is on Earth. God's presence here is in the person of the Holy Spirit. Through Him spiritual access is provided into the sanctuary in heaven, where are God the Father and Jesus Christ.

- The symbolism of Christ being a rock (representing His eternal deity, on which He is building the church which is His Body) is different from that of Him being exalted to be the stone chosen by God to be the foundation of the spiritual house of God.

- Christ is in heaven, serving as high priest over God's house. This is referred to as our hope. He presents the people's offerings to His God and Father and makes them acceptable.

- Holding fast to belief in this hope is central to the conditions for believers continuing to be God's house.

- Those in the house are urged to continually draw near into the sanctuary in heaven to offer their spiritual sacrifices through Christ.

- If these then are the prerequisites of being in God's house today, each of us as a disciple of the Lord Jesus should ask ourselves "Am I part of that house, or am I missing something"?

"Send forth your light and your truth,
let them guide me;
let them bring me to your holy mountain,
to the place where you dwell."
(Psalm 43:3 NIV)

Discovering God's Church

The Churches of God—Where God is Calling Disciples to Gather to Serve Him

"the church of God which He purchased with His own blood" (Acts 20:28)

12.

What is a Church?

"When you come together as a church ..." (1 Corinthians 11:18)

As we saw earlier, commonly when people talk about a church these days they are referring to a religious building, a place of worship. We may be encouraged to "worship at a church near you," or talk about "going to church" or constructing a new church. In fact the buildings themselves often have signs labelling them as churches. But this is not the Bible meaning of the word.

Ekklesia

The Bible word for church, *"ekklesia,"* meaning people called out to be together, is used in several contexts. We have already looked at its use in connection with "the church the Body of Christ". Israel in the wilderness is referred to in Acts 7:38 as *"the church in the wilderness"* [12]. It is also used for secular gatherings (e.g. Acts 19:39). But the most common usage is of local gatherings of God's people, where the term "church of God" is used, to denote that it is God who has called them together. This is the only use in the New Testament in which the word occurs both in the singular (e.g. 1 Corinthians 1:2) and the plural (e.g. 1 Corinthians 11:16). Each church of God was identified with a particular place, such as Jerusalem (Galatians 1:13), Corinth (1 Corinthians 1:2), and Thessalonica (1 Thessalonians 1:1). In Jerusalem, on the Day of Pentecost, the disciples who were baptized and added to the approximately one hundred and twenty who were already gathered together had been called together by God, as "the church of God" in that place.

Why does church matter?

There is certainly no shortage of Christian church groups and denominations to choose from these days. A believer in many countries who wishes to gather

---

12   Translated as "church" in the King James Version, "assembly" in the NIV, and "congregation" in the NKJV and NASB.

with other believers can find an almost unlimited variety. Is this a good thing? It certainly caters to various preferences, cultures, and traditions. People are free to choose as they like on the basis of convenience of location, ethnic background, the pastor, the programs that are offered, where friends and family members attend, and so on. There is a widespread view that the actual basis on which Christians gather together is not that important since, after all, they are all members of that one "true church," which is Christ's Body.

Some believers may say that it is not that important whether a Christian belongs to a church or not. If, as some say, the essence of the Christian faith is the personal relationship between a believer and Jesus Christ, then any church affiliation is secondary; it is there primarily as an option to support their personal Christian walk. Thus, they would argue, Christians should feel free to come and go as they please. But is this in fact what the Scriptures teach, or are we again missing something?

We do not have to study our Bibles for very long before we realize that living out our Christian lives necessarily includes our relationships with other believers. For example, while the well-known verse John 3:16 tells us about how we obtain salvation, a corresponding verse in 1 John chapter 3 links that with the importance of our relationship with each other: *"This is His commandment: that we believe in the name of His Son Jesus Christ and love one another, as He commanded us"* (1 John 3:23).

Loving one another is one of the foremost commands to the Christian. Jesus said that this was how other people would know that they were His disciples (John 13:35). We cannot fulfill that command by staying apart from other Christians or by picking and choosing those whom we will gather with just to suit ourselves.

What should the church be called?

Today churches are called by various names, perhaps reflecting their denominational association, community location, or some other characteristic. Sometimes contests are held to find a name for a new church. However, what matters is not what we may choose to call it but what God calls it. If *"ekklesia"* refers to the fact that God has called disciples together into His churches, then it is God who must put His name on them, just as He put His name on His people Israel in Old Testament times. [13]

---

13 He also put His name on the city of Jerusalem: *"Jerusalem, the city where I have chosen for Myself to put My name"* (1 Kings 11:36). That is what made it the holy city, the city of God.

For this reason the name that was given to local churches in the New Testament was "church of God." Each was God's church; otherwise, it would have had no right to take that name for itself. God puts His name on something only when it belongs to Him and meets His requirements.

Various other expressions using the word "church" occur in various places:

- The church in a house (e.g. Romans 16:5; 1 Corinthians 16:19; Colossians 4:15), referring to one or more homes where the saints in the church of God in the town met.

- "*The church of the living God*" (1 Timothy 3:15), referring to the house of God, as discussed in the last section.

- "*The church throughout all Judea and Galilee and Samaria*" (Acts 9:31), referring to the aggregate of all those in the churches of God in those regions.

- "*The churches of the saints*" (1 Corinthians 14:33), emphasizing that it is saints who make up the churches.

- "*The churches of Christ*" (Romans 16:16), also referring to local gatherings of those in churches of God, emphasizing the character and authority of Christ over them (as seen in Revelation 1:12,13).

God calls us to church

When the apostle Paul came for the first time to the city of Corinth in Achaia he had a lot of opposition. He was tempted to leave and go elsewhere, but the Lord told him to stay because "*I have many people in this city*" (Acts 18:10). Because of his work there, "*the church of God which is at Corinth*" came into existence (1 Corinthians 1:2; 2 Corinthians 2:1). It was established by disciples responding in obedience to the call of God. This was the same basis as every other church of God had been and would be in the future. That was the church to which he wrote his two epistles.

Different callings

In his first epistle, Paul used the word "call" four times in the first nine verses, and each time it had a somewhat different meaning. Firstly, he mentioned his own individual *calling* to be an apostle: "*Paul, called as an apostle of Jesus Christ*" (verse 1). This referred to God having summoned him to his particular ministry, as described in Acts 13:2,3, although He had predetermined it from eternity (Acts 13:2,3; Galatians 1:15; 2 Timothy 1:8,9).

Secondly, he told the church that God had *called* them to be saints (that is, His holy ones): *"To the church of God which is at Corinth, to those who have been sanctified in Christ Jesus, saints by calling"* (verse 2). The word "saints" is always used in this collective sense in the New Testament; we never read of an individual saint.

Thirdly, he mentioned that they were linked with saints in other places, *"with all who in every place call on the name of our Lord Jesus Christ, their Lord and ours"* (verses 2,3). This expression "call on the name of the Lord" is referring to their spiritual activity, and occurs throughout Scripture, beginning in Genesis 4:26. It is used to refer to those in the churches of God whom Paul himself persecuted (Acts 9:21), and was the hallmark of those gathered in churches of God.

Finally, he told them that God had *"called"* them into a fellowship: *"God is faithful, by whom you were called into the fellowship of His Son, Jesus Christ our Lord"* (verse 9 NKJV). The Greek work for *call,* meaning "to summon," is the same word as the one used to call someone by their own name. In effect, God had called them out by name. It was a personal calling.

Note that in verse 9 it is *"the fellowship of,"* not "fellowship with," as some translations put it. The definite article "the" is included in the Greek original text, making it clear that it was not referring to their individual fellowship *"with"* Jesus Christ (1 John 1:6), but to a defined community of disciples. This is as it was with the original church in Jerusalem; they *"continued steadfastly in … the fellowship …"* (Acts 2:42—the definite article is included there also). Therefore, these saints in Corinth had been called into the same fellowship as those in the churches of God elsewhere. God was faithful; He had committed Himself to them, and He expected them in turn to commit themselves to Him (and to each other). It was a partnership, a community, of separated believers which belonged to the Lord Jesus.

As followers of the Lord Jesus, we can see that the choice of church gathering is not really up to us. Since it is God who calls disciples together for divine activity, we should look for and respond to His call. Casual fellowship, shopping around (or hopping around) from one church to another, is not the scriptural way. It is the people who form the church. Disciples are therefore expected to belong to it, to "be" the church, to commit themselves to it and not to leave it (except to move to another such church of God). If God calls us into it, He will not later call us out of it (Romans 11:29).

This is a very different concept of church than is prevalent in the world today. But Scripture shows us that it is the Lord's way, as is evident from the first church that was brought into existence in Jerusalem almost two thousand years ago, which we will look at now.

13.

The First Church of God

"A great persecution began against the church in Jerusalem" (Acts 8:1)
"I persecuted the church of God" (1 Corinthians 15:9)

The churches of God that were established in New Testament times serve as the model for us today. [14] The first century model is applicable to the twenty-first century. The first church of God was in Jerusalem, the very city in which the Lord Jesus had been crucified and buried. It had been the destination of the earthly people of God in the Old Testament, and it became the starting point for the people of God in New Testament times. Because it was the first church and set the pattern, it is particularly instructive. [15]

The church in Jerusalem

Let's examine this church of God in Jerusalem. It came into existence on the day of Pentecost about ten days after the Lord Jesus had returned to heaven. He had spent the time between His resurrection and His final departure instructing His apostles: *"... appearing to them over a period of forty days and speaking of the things concerning the kingdom of God"* (Acts 1:3). We are not told the details of what He said to them, but we can infer it very clearly from the Acts of the Apostles and the epistles.

Towards the end of that period, the Lord gave them what is often referred to as the Great Commission: *"Go therefore and make disciples of all the nations, baptiz-*

---

14 The early chapters of the book of Acts are far more than just a historical account of what happened in those days; they serve as a pattern for us to follow. While some things were undoubtedly only relevant to those times, what is recorded for us in Scripture generally applies for us to practice today, even though we live centuries later.

15 This is often the case; the first occurrence of something in Scripture generally sets a pattern for what follows, which is why the book of Genesis is often called "the seed-plot of the Bible."

ing them in the name of the Father and the Son and the Holy Spirit, teaching them to observe all that I commanded you; and lo, I am with you always, even to the end of the age" (Matthew 28:19,20). He told them to wait in Jerusalem until they received *"power from on high"* (Luke 24:49), referring to the Holy Spirit. When Pentecost came, *"they were all together in one place"* (Acts 2:1), and the Spirit was poured out on them. Then they began to carry out exactly what the Lord had told them to do.

A crowd gathered. Peter stood up and preached to them. About three thousand people responded in faith to his preaching. They were then immediately baptized in water and were added to those one hundred and twenty (or so) disciples who were already together (Acts 1:15). And they continued from then on with them:

> *"So then, those who had received his word were baptized; and that day there were added about three thousand souls. They were continually devoting themselves to the apostles' teaching and to fellowship, to the breaking of bread and to prayer"* (Acts 2:41,42).

This is how the church of God in Jerusalem came into existence. One by one disciples were made, were baptized by immersion, and were added to their number. Even though three thousand of them were added on that one day, they were individually added to what had been the smaller group that already existed. This was not a group merger.

Being added to the Lord

We are told that, as disciples were being added to the church, the Lord was adding them to Himself. It says they were *"added to the Lord"* (Acts 5:14 NKJV). And so we are introduced to the position of being *"in the Lord"* (Greek: *en kurioo*), which occurs frequently in the epistles. This is a distinct term, different from our position of being "in Christ" or "in Christ Jesus," such as, *"If anyone is in Christ, he is a new creature"* (2 Corinthians 5:17). That term refers to our eternal position related solely to the work of Christ on our behalf. Those who are *"in"* Christ can never be *"out of"* Christ; it does not depend on them. It applies to all who have been eternally saved.

But being "in the Lord" goes beyond that. It requires that a disciple continuously acknowledge Christ's mastery over their lives—His lordship. Maintaining that relationship therefore does depend on their on-going obedience and submission on Earth to His teaching.

It is important for us to notice that these disciples were being joined in two directions—to the Lord and to each other. This was essential to their oneness, just as Israel's oneness as God's holy nation hinged on the two greatest commandments of loving the Lord and also loving each other (Matthew 22:36–40), as we looked at in chapter 10.

Continuing steadfastly

Acts 2:42 describes the activities of that first church of God in Jerusalem. As distinct from the three one-time actions of each new convert which are described in verse 41 (gladly receiving his preaching for salvation, being baptized, and being added together), verse 42 refers to four things that they all continued to do together. This was the church in action.

1. The first one mentioned is the doctrinal basis of their gathering—"*the apostles' teaching*"—what the Lord had instructed them to teach in its entirety. Adhering to that was what they had in common. If they did not get the teaching right, nothing else would be right. The Lord Jesus had instructed His apostles to teach the newly-baptized disciples "*all that I commanded you*" (Matthew 28:20). They were not to leave anything out. This included much more than telling people how they could be eternally saved through faith in Christ and how to live individual Christian lives. It certainly included those things, but it also included their need to be baptized, their need to be added to a church of God, and how to live their on-going lives of obedience and service as part of that church.

2. The second thing they continued in was "*the fellowship.*" [16] This was the defined community to which they and those in future churches of God would all belong as they adhered to that same teaching. The apostles and the others who were originally "*all with one accord in one place*" (Acts 2:2) were a community. They had been called together by the Lord to one place, for one purpose. The others who were added became part of that community. God intended that they serve Him together. They were made individually by Him, but made for fellowship with each other.

3. The third activity that this community engaged in was "*the breaking of bread.*" This refers to the keeping of the Lord's Supper, the regular remembrance of the Lord Jesus in the bread and wine, as He had commanded the apostles.

4. The fourth activity was "*the prayers*"—gatherings for prayer.

---

16 Note that in the Greek text the definite article "the" is expressly used with all four of these ongoing church activities, although this is not reflected in all English versions. It was "the apostles' teaching," "the fellowship," "the breaking of bread," and "the prayers." These were not things that they just did separately as individuals. They did them as a church, as is made explicit for example in Acts 12:5: "*Peter was kept in the prison, but prayer for him was being made fervently by the church to God.*"

Church life in the early days

The verses that follow in Acts chapter 2 describe what life was like in that early Jerusalem church:

> *"Everyone kept feeling a sense of awe; and many wonders and signs were taking place through the apostles. And all those who had believed were together and had all things in common; and they began selling their property and possessions and were sharing them with all, as anyone might have need. Day by day continuing with one mind in the temple, and breaking bread from house to house, they were taking their meals together with gladness and sincerity of heart, praising God and having favor with all the people. And the Lord was adding to their number day by day those who were being saved."* (Acts 2:43–47)

The highlights of this description include the following:

- Their awe of God, which kept them humble; they took these matters seriously.

- The evidence of God's presence in signs and wonders, which provided necessary confirmation in those days (when they had no New Testament Scriptures to rely on) that what they were doing was of the Lord (Hebrews 2:4).

- Their togetherness and sharing, meeting each other's needs—a true sense of community.

- Their steadfastness—continuing every day in their devotedness.

- Their gladness—praising God and bearing positive testimony in public.

- Their growth—the Lord was adding new disciples. Only growth that comes from God is good growth (1 Corinthians 3:7).

This was a fully functioning church of God. They were a tightly knit and devoted community. These were marvellous days. But would these things continue, or was this just a unique case? And how much of what happened then applies to us now? This is what we need to turn our attention to next.

14.

Establishing a Pattern

"The things which you have heard from me in the presence of many witnesses, entrust these to faithful men who will be able to teach others also." (2 Timothy 2:2)

Since the experience of the first church of God in Jerusalem is intended to set a pattern for us now, even though we live almost two thousand years later, what is that pattern? Let us examine the elements that were involved in that first church in Jerusalem to determine how applicable they are.

First: Salvation

The new disciples first gladly received the word that Peter was preaching. The first spiritual event in any person's life must be coming into a personal relationship with Jesus Christ—to receive eternal salvation through faith in Him and to acknowledge Him as their Lord. God calls people to Himself through the preaching of the gospel from the Word of God (2 Thessalonians 2:14). He uses existing disciples to do that, as Peter did at Pentecost, and the whole church did subsequently: *"Those who had been scattered went about preaching the word"* (Acts 8:4). And so evangelism—spreading the good news—is a vital part of the service and activity of a church of God. Without it, there cannot be believers in Christ and disciples to form God's church.

A church with unsaved people in it cannot be a church of God. Since a church of God is the result of God calling people together, it can only consist of people who have first responded to God's call to them in the gospel. This then is the first requirement—only believers in Jesus Christ can be in a church of God. But it is not the only one.

Second: Baptism

Those newly saved disciples were then immediately baptized. The Lord had instructed that this be done, into the name of the Father and of the Son and of the Holy Spirit (Matthew 28:19). This was a baptism by immersion in water, as is evident from the later case of Philip and the eunuch from Ethiopia: *"He ordered the chariot to stop; and they both went down into the water, Philip as well as the eunuch, and he baptized him. When they came up out of the water, the Spirit of the Lord snatched Philip away"* (Acts 8:38,39).

In fact, the word baptism comes directly from the Greek word *"baptizo,"* which means "to immerse." It was a common word, used for such things as dying cloth. The baptism of these disciples was a public acknowledgement of their inner spiritual experience, and of their identification with Christ in His death to sin and in His resurrection in order to *"walk in newness of life"* (Romans 6:4) [17].

When Peter began preaching to Gentiles, he first went to the city of Caesarea in response to a call to introduce this new gospel to the centurion Cornelius and his household. As he was speaking to them on that occasion, when it became apparent that those hearing had believed the gospel and received the Holy Spirit, Peter commanded them to be baptized. This shows us that being baptized is not optional but is a command, just as is the corresponding command to make and baptize new disciples.

Being baptized is the first public act of obedience that new disciples carry out to their newly found Lord. Jesus set the example Himself by being baptized by John in the Jordan River *"to fulfill all righteousness"* (Matthew 3:15). This emphasizes that a disciple's baptism is not part of how he or she becomes eternally saved, since that is by faith and confession alone (Ephesians 2:8,9; Romans 10:9),[18] but it is the response to the Lord by someone who has already been saved. Peter called it *"the answer of a good conscience toward God"* (1 Peter 3:21 NKJV).

In the Old Testament we are given an illustration of our baptism in the experience of Israel passing through the Red Sea: *"Our fathers were all under the cloud and all passed through the sea; and all were baptized into Moses in the cloud and in the sea"* (1 Corinthians 10:1,2). The people had been slaves in Egypt under the domination of Pharaoh. But God had redeemed them, by means of the blood of the Passover lambs, and separated them from the Egyptian people (Exodus

---

17 In those early days, baptism was also a public declaration by Jewish believers of their allegiance to Jesus the Messiah, whom their nation had just rejected and crucified. They were setting themselves apart from what their leaders had done. When the gospel began being proclaimed to Gentiles, we see the current order: receiving the Holy Spirit at salvation, with baptism by immersion to follow (Acts 10:44-48).

18 The error of "baptismal regeneration"—that a person must be baptized in water to be eternally saved—is what led to the baptism of newborn infants in the centuries following the New Testament. This was eventually changed to sprinkling for safety reasons (and eventually led to the use of "holy water").

8:23). They were now about to embark on a new life together, under the leadership of Moses, and they had to be cut off from their old life in Egypt by passing through the Red Sea. This illustrates why we as disciples go through the water of baptism—to symbolize the end of our old life of living to ourselves and the domination of sin, and the start of a new life under the lordship of Jesus Christ (Romans 6:3–7). And so, baptism has two parts to it—going down into the water and coming up out of the water. The first symbolizes burial of the old self as being dead to sin; the second symbolizes being raised to live a new life to Christ in the power of the Holy Spirit.

The act of baptism itself involves three aspects—by, in, and into. It is performed "*by*" another disciple; it is "*in*" water; and it is "*into*" the name (authority) of the Father and of the Son and of the Holy Spirit (Matthew 28:19). Note that it is "name" in the singular, because of the unity of the godhead.

What we are baptized "*into*" is important. Not only the words that are said at the time are important, but what is understood by them. For example, when Paul encountered some disciples in Ephesus, he discovered that they had not been baptized into that name but rather into John's baptism. He told them they needed to be baptized again, this time into [Greek: '*eis*'] the name of the Lord Jesus (Acts 19:1–5). And they were. To be baptized into the name of the Lord Jesus is to be placed completely at His disposal, as Lord of our lives, in accordance with Matthew 28:19.

Third: Addition

The third thing that happened to those new disciples at Pentecost in Jerusalem was that they were added to the disciples already gathered there, although they greatly outnumbered them—approximately three thousand to about one hundred and twenty. But additions are not in groups; each disciple had to be added individually to the group already together.

They did not "join" or become members of a church. (In fact, it is only in respect to the church the Body of Christ that we are called "members" e.g. Romans 12:4; 1 Corinthians 12:18,20,25; Ephesians 3:6). God does not want us merely to attend church or to join ourselves to a church, but to be added to His church, to become part of it. It was the existing group of disciples that added them, as directed by the Lord.

Those disciples, which included the twelve apostles, *"were all with one accord in one place"* (Acts 2:1 NKJV). This is a significant expression; not only were they in one location but they also had a unity of purpose. They were waiting, as the Lord had told them to do before He left them: *"Gathering them together, He commanded them not to leave Jerusalem, but to wait for what the Father had promised,*

'Which,' He said, 'you heard of from Me; for John baptized with water, but you will be baptized with the Holy Spirit not many days from now'" (Acts 1:4–6).

The people *were* the church. They were "*ekklesia,*" a group of people called out by God and called together for His purpose in that place. At Pentecost they became the church of God in Jerusalem. The addition of these three thousand new disciples was a distinct step for each one of them, and it meant leaving behind whatever they had been part of previously. They could not form the church of God and still be attached to something that was contrary to it.

The Scripture goes on to say that it was actually the Lord who was adding them, and they were being added to Him: "*the Lord added to the church*" (Acts 2:47 NKJV) and "*believers were increasingly added to the Lord*" (Acts 5:14 NKJV; see also Acts 11:24). As a result of being added to the Lord, their relationship to Him is described in several places as being "*in the Lord,*" as we looked at earlier. And one benefit of this was that they became part of the "*holy temple in the Lord*" (Ephesians 2:21) which, as we saw in the last section, refers to the house of God.

Being added to a church of God involves making a commitment to the Lord Jesus and also to those in it. It is like a partnership, and that is what is meant by the words "*the fellowship*" in Acts 2:42. Casual or occasional fellowship is not an option that is offered.

Just as disciples are added to the church, sadly it is also possible for them to be put away from it [19]. For example, in his first epistle to the church at Corinth, in chapter 5, the apostle Paul wrote about the need for them to put someone out of the church because of serious sin. This shows that a church of God is something that a baptized disciple must not only be consciously added to, but may also have to be removed from. It is not just a gathering that exists to be attended or casually joined. The church does not automatically consist of all believers in a certain town. They must be added to it, and they must continue steadfastly in it. Gathering together for service is at the very heart of what a church is.

And so the church of God in Jerusalem came into existence that Pentecost day and consisted of saved, baptized, and added disciples of the Lord Jesus. And that is also the pattern for us. We have no basis to change it. At this initial stage it was co-extensive with the church the Body of Christ—all who were born again and so were members of that Body were also baptized in water and in the local church. That is the way it should be. But sadly that did not last for very long.

---

19 This is one of the differences between a church of God and the church the Body of Christ.

On-going service

The first three steps that we have just examined—salvation, baptism, and addition—all involved actions by individuals. In each case, the disciple made a decision to do it, and each step only had to take place once. It resulted in them being part of a defined group, the church of God, and from then on their individual actions had to be guided by what they were part of.

The order of these three things is very important. Being baptized should not come before salvation; that is what led later to the practice of baptizing or sprinkling infants. Nor should being added come before salvation; the church is not for unbelievers, and churches should not have mixed congregations of believers and unbelievers. Also, addition to the church should not come before the commitment of baptism.

Acts 2:42 then describes how they began to participate in regular collective service. It included four on-going activities that were core functions of the church. Just as the sequence in which the three events in verse 41 occur is important, so is the sequence in which these four are mentioned. When we get these steps out of sequence, we get into difficulty. This sequence represents God's divine order.

Continuing in the apostles' teaching

It says firstly that they devoted themselves to "the apostles' teaching." A disciple by definition is one who learns, and then follows what he or she is learning. It is a never-ending process. People are not added to a church of God because of what they already know, but because of what they are willing to learn and to do.

The apostles taught everything that the Lord Jesus had taught them, just as He had instructed them to do (Matthew 28:20). It was a complete doctrine, and it formed the basis of the fellowship of which they were now a part. They did not come together for fellowship and then determine what teaching to follow. They did not form a community despite differences of doctrine. The doctrine was the basis of it all. Later, as the churches expanded to far off regions, it was a priority to maintain that uniform teaching, which was the very basis of their identity, because it had come from the Lord Jesus in the first place. Therefore, the apostles' teaching is just as relevant for us in the twenty-first century, and it continues to be the basis on which disciples should gather and serve God. We are all responsible for what we do with the apostles' teaching.

Sometimes we hear it said that doctrine does not really matter. And sometimes we hear that we should downplay doctrine because it has tended to lead to divisions among Christians. But doctrine is vital; it is the whole basis of our coming together in service for God. Doctrine is not just theory. It is what the Lord has told us to do, and so it is extremely practical. It explains to us what we should be doing to please Him. We cannot just relegate it to lesser importance.

This emphasis on the apostles' teaching inevitably meant that on-going teaching of the Word of God became an essential element in the activity of churches of God. For this purpose, teachers were raised up by the Holy Spirit (Romans 12:6,7) to follow on from the apostles. For example, the apostle Paul stressed to the young man Timothy the importance of continual sound teaching, and of correcting wrong teaching (1 Timothy 1:3; 4:11; 6:2).

Apollos was a Jewish man who was knowledgeable and eloquent in the Scriptures. When he came to Ephesus he spoke accurately what he knew, but his understanding was limited, *"being acquainted only with the baptism of John"* (Acts 18:25,26). A woman and her husband in the church there, Priscilla and Aquila, heard him speaking in the synagogue. They took him aside *"and explained to him the way of God more accurately."* As a result, Apollos came into the church of God in Ephesus, and later became an effective teacher in the church of God in Corinth (1 Corinthians 1:12; 3:6). Despite Apollos' reputation, Priscilla and Aquila were not afraid to approach him to teach him more of the way of God. It was clearly important to them. And he was obviously not above learning it and putting it into practice. That is a lovely example of the spirit of discipleship. Accurate and complete teaching of the Scriptures is vital for disciples in churches of God.

Continuing in the fellowship

The fellowship (community) that these disciples were added to (Acts 2:42) is described in the apostle Paul's letter to the Corinthians: *"God is faithful, by whom you were called into the fellowship of His Son, Jesus Christ our Lord"* (1 Corinthians 1:9 NKJV). As we saw previously, this is a defined fellowship. The definite article shows that there is only one.

God desires unity among His people, as it reflects His own character. We live in a very individualistic age, in a society where personal differences and individual rights are considered very important. God has made us all different from one another, but He has a common purpose for us all. He is working to bring all believers into conformity with His Son (Romans 8:29). Meanwhile, He desires to unite us in our lives and service for Him. He calls us into a community that belongs to His Son. And that leaves no room for having an attitude of independence or isolation, either in our personal lives or in our church lives.

For disciples in churches of God to be His house on Earth, His "holy temple," the individual churches must be *"fitted together"* (Ephesians 2:21; *"joined together"* NKJV) in the Lord. This fellowship must be based on the teaching of the Lord

Jesus through His apostles. Any union or association that is on any other basis cannot qualify.

This partnership of saints and churches was shown in several practical ways in New Testament times. We saw earlier how the saints in the church in Jerusalem spent time with each other, supported each other, and met each other's practical needs. Even when the community became more widespread, this kind of fellowship continued. For example, the disciples in Antioch decided to send relief to their brethren and sisters in Judea many miles away, because of the famine there (Acts 11:29).

The inter-relationships that characterize the Body of Christ are intended to be seen within each local church of God. It is in these close quarters of community living where it can be the most challenging. We do not choose our brothers and sisters in the Lord—He does that—but the local church is the setting where our love for one another has the greatest opportunity to be worked out in practice. It has been said that church life is the laboratory where we actually learn to be Christ-like rather than just talking about it.

Therefore, the pattern for us is that the churches of God must be a community, with the same teaching and with practical interaction and inter-dependency. Independent churches cannot be "churches of God."

Continuing in the breaking of bread

The new church then devoted itself to the regular remembrance of the Lord Jesus in the emblems of bread and wine. The Lord Jesus had originated this means for His disciples to remember Him back in the upper room (Luke 22:19), and He gave a special revelation of it later to the apostle Paul:

> *"For I received from the Lord that which I also delivered to you, that the Lord Jesus in the night in which He was betrayed took bread; and when He had given thanks, He broke it and said, 'This is My body, which is for you; do this in remembrance of Me.' In the same way He took the cup also after supper, saying, 'This cup is the new covenant in My blood; do this, as often as you drink it, in remembrance of Me. For as often as you eat this bread and drink the cup, you proclaim the Lord's death until He comes'"* (1 Corinthians 11:23-26).

In the previous chapter, Paul had described it as a communion, a sharing: *"Is not the cup of blessing which we bless a sharing in the blood of Christ? Is not the bread which we break a sharing in the body of Christ?"* (1 Corinthians 10:16). He also referred to these emblems as *"the cup of the Lord"* (verse 21), the *"Lord's table"* (verse 21), and as *"the Lord's supper"* (11:20).

It was the church that kept this remembrance. They came together as a church for this purpose (1 Corinthians 11:18). It is not prescribed as something for individual believers to engage in. Keeping this remembrance just as individual believers would be getting this third step in Acts 2:42 ahead of addition to the church (the third step in the previous verse). In fact, because these Corinthian saints were abusing this remembrance, Paul said to them, *"Do you despise the church of God?"* (1 Corinthians 11:22). They were acting in a way that damaged the harmony of those with whom they had been called together.

The breaking of bread in Acts 2:42 is different from just eating meals together, which the church in Jerusalem also did, as verse 46 shows: *"Day by day continuing with one mind in the temple, and breaking bread from house to house, they were taking their meals together with gladness and sincerity of heart"* (Acts 2:46). It was a particular spiritual activity of remembering the Lord Jesus in the way He had shown.

Paul went on in chapter 11 to emphasize the importance of proper conduct and attitude at the Lord's Supper. He clearly differentiated it from just sharing food together, which is what the Corinthians were doing: *"When you meet together, it is not to eat the Lord's Supper, for in your eating each one takes his own supper first; and one is hungry and another is drunk"* (1 Corinthians 11:20,21). He told them to examine themselves before they ate to make sure they were properly discerning the significance of the emblems (because they were, in fact, only emblems); they represented the body and blood of the Lord Jesus. Because of this wrong conduct and attitude, God had been bringing judgment on them. Some of them were sick and some had even died. Obviously, the Lord takes His supper very seriously, and so should we.

In the order of activities in Acts 2:42, the breaking of bread comes before the prayers. It is focussed on giving to God, and that must always come before asking for ourselves. Further worship of thanksgiving and praise follows this remembrance; it is all collective worship to God by the holy priesthood. The link between the two is seen in Hebrews chapter 10, which (as we saw earlier) describes those in the house of God drawing near to Him to worship: *"Therefore, brethren, since we have confidence to enter the holy place by the blood of Jesus, by a new and living way which He inaugurated for us through the veil, that is, His flesh, and since we have a great priest over the house of God, let us draw near with a sincere heart in full assurance of faith"* (Hebrews 10:19–22). The two bases on which we are able to come into the presence of God are *"the veil, that is His flesh"* and *"the blood of Jesus."* It is His flesh and His blood that are symbolized in the bread and wine that we partake of in the act of remembering.

The first day of the week was the day that the disciples gathered for this activity: *"We sailed from Philippi after the days of Unleavened Bread, and came to them at Troas within five days; and there we stayed seven days. On the first day of the week, when we were gathered together to break bread, Paul began talking to them, intending to leave the next day, and he prolonged his message until midnight"* (Acts 20:6,7). Paul had to stay at Troas for a whole week on his journey from Philippi to Jerusalem in order to be there for the breaking of bread. His speaking the word to the church came after that; the breaking of bread came first.

The disciples had discontinued the keeping of the Sabbath, which had been such a vital observance under the old covenant (Colossians 2:16,17). Instead they met on the first day of the week (John 19:19,26), which was the day of the Lord's resurrection (John 20:1), and it signified the new order of things that had been brought about by that pivotal event.

Even in the Old Testament, the principle that God's things must come first had been clearly established. This was seen, for example, in the instructions about firstborn sons and first fruits of crops (Exodus 22:29; 23:19). The first things were devoted to God. We see this principle at work in the sin of Achan, who took the spoil of the defeat of Jericho, which was Israel's first conquest in the land of Canaan. Jericho was under a ban because its spoils belonged to God, and Achan paid for his mistake with his life (Joshua 6:17–19,24). We need to learn that we are expected to firstly give to God what belongs to Him, which is the worship of our hearts. We do it on the first day of the week, and first thing on that day.

We can see therefore that the weekly remembrance of the Lord Jesus in the symbols of bread and wine, and the related collective worship by the holy priesthood, on the first day of each week, is the pattern for each church of God today. Other service can then follow afterward.

Why is it not for any believer?

When the Lord Jesus was on Earth, a large number of people believed in Him (John 2:23; 10:42). But it was to His apostles and disciples that He said *"Do not be afraid, little flock, for your Father has chosen gladly to give you the kingdom"* (Luke 12:32). It was with the apostles that He initiated His remembrance in the bread and the wine (Luke 22:14). And it was to the apostles that He gave instruction about the kingdom of God after His resurrection (Acts 1:1–3). How were other believers to also have a part in these things? It was only by them aligning themselves with those apostles—with their teaching and their fellowship. That is what the rest of the hundred and twenty did who waited and prayed with them until the Holy Spirit came (Acts 1:13–15). That is what the three thousand did who heard and believed the gospel on the Day of Pentecost (Acts 2:41,42). That is what Saul of Tarsus did when he was converted (Acts 9:19,26,27). The little flock was becoming bigger. As it grew, and as Gentiles were added to it, as the Lord Jesus had spoken of in John 10:16, it remained one flock, with one shepherd. It was the flock of God (1 Peter 5:2,3).

These privileges are not automatically given to us as believers by virtue of salvation alone. It is available to all of us, but first we must be baptized and added to the church that is "of God", according to the apostles' teaching.

Continuing in the prayers

The last activity listed in Acts 2:42 refers to church gatherings for prayer—"*the prayers*". These were in addition to the saints praying individually or in groups. It was, and still is, a vital activity of a church of God. As the Lord Jesus said, quoting Isaiah 56:7, *"My house shall be called a house of prayer for all nations"* (Mark 11:17). Even before the Day of Pentecost, those who were together were devoting themselves to prayer (Acts 1:13,14). Collective prayer was a way of life for them.

We see an example of the effect of united prayer by the church in the case of Peter's rescue from prison, during a time of great persecution of the disciples in Jerusalem: *"So Peter was kept in the prison, but prayer for him was being made fervently by the church to God"* (Acts 12:5). Peter was released miraculously, by an angel coming to free him. Then he went to one of the places where the church was continuing to gather in prayer. They almost could not believe that their prayers had been answered.

Agreeing in prayer is important, as the Lord Jesus Himself explained: *"I say to you, that if two of you agree on earth about anything that they may ask, it shall be done for them by My Father who is in heaven"* (Matthew 18:19).

Hebrews chapter 4 indicates that the prayers of God's collective people also involve the priestly work of Christ. He is described there as the man who totally understands our needs and feelings. Because of Him, God's throne is for us a throne of grace.

In prayer we address our requests to God as our Father, since He is the giver of all good things (James 1:17), and we offer them in the name (authority) of the Lord Jesus Christ (John 16:24). In addition to making requests, however, the scope of the prayers of God's people is extensive: *"I urge that entreaties and prayers, petitions and thanksgivings, be made on behalf of all men"* (1 Timothy 2:1).

The prayers of the saints are pictured in Revelation 5:8 as golden censers (bowls) full of incense, with a beautiful fragrance that constantly rises up to God. While disciples may gather to pray for particular things at particular times on Earth, it is as though their prayers are all collected in bowls, and the sweet smell constantly rises to God for His enjoyment. He is not bound by restrictions of time or location, as we are.

And so we see that the regular gathering of disciples in a church of God for prayer is a vital part of their on-going activity. It is part of the pattern for us today.

The order of Acts 2:42

Just as we saw earlier in the chapter that the sequence of things in verse 41 is vital, so is the sequence of verse 42. Problems develop when we change God's order of things.

For example, if we put the fellowship before the teaching—that is, if we do not gather based on the teaching—then the gathering itself becomes more important than the teaching. This can lead a church to adapting or adjusting doctrine to preserve itself as an organization. That is what the Reformers of the fourteenth to sixteenth Centuries claimed the church was doing at that time.

Then, for example, if we put the breaking of bread before the fellowship, we include in the Lord's Supper those who are not in churches of God. If we put the prayers (or other service for God, such as preaching the gospel) before the breaking of bread, God is not being given His part first.

In the pattern that has been left for us, this divine order is vital. But was it continued as the churches began to multiply and as disciples began to spread out geographically? Let's look at that question next.

15.

Reproducing the Pattern

"And so I direct in all the churches." (1 Corinthians 7:17)

Initially there was just one church of God, in Jerusalem, although it often gathered in multiple locations—various homes, and also public places such as the Solomon's porch area of the temple grounds. But eventually many churches of God were established throughout the Roman Empire as the community expanded. It also became more culturally diverse, as Gentiles were added. But it remained as one community. Its united adherence to the full teaching of the faith remained paramount.

Throughout the book of the Acts of the Apostles, as well as the epistles, it is noteworthy how diligent the disciples were in maintaining this unity. It would have been very easy for them to have become fragmented and separate, especially with long distances between them, limited methods of communication, and the cultural differences between Gentiles and Jews. But they worked hard at it by various means, such as visitation, written epistles, an elders' and apostles' conference, mutual prayer, and the sending of practical support to those in need.

The persecution

The persecution of the disciples by the Jews (such as Saul of Tarsus) became so severe that almost the whole church at Jerusalem fled in various directions (Acts 8:1). Disciples became known initially as "the Way" (Acts 9:2; 24:14) and were regarded as a sect. Later they become known as "Christians" (Acts 11:26)—that is, followers of the Messiah. However the apostles did not leave Jerusalem, and so all these other saints were now on their own as they established churches in other places. The church in Jerusalem became a lot smaller in a hurry.

First of all, a new development started in Samaria, a region a few miles north of Jerusalem, where Philip the evangelist had gone (Acts 8:5–12). People were being saved and baptized, and so the apostles Peter and John went to Samaria to link the group there with the existing ones in Jerusalem and elsewhere in the region of Judea. Maintaining this unity of teaching and communications was vital, and it was up to the apostles to lay the foundation of the uniform teaching. The churches in Samaria were not a new movement; they were becoming a new part of the existing fellowship.

Meanwhile, back in Jerusalem, an eager young orthodox Jew from Tarsus by the name of Saul, who was already a member of the elite Pharisees, began a personal campaign to stamp out these disciples in churches of God. He imprisoned them and sentenced them to death. He thought that what they were doing was sacrilegious. It says that he made havoc of the church (Acts 8:3). He himself said later that he *"persecuted the church of God"* (1 Corinthians 15:9). But Christ said about it at the time: *"Why are you persecuting Me?"* (Acts 9:4). It is clear that Christ takes the church of God very personally.

After Jerusalem, he intended to track these disciples down as far as Damascus, about a hundred miles to the northeast, but he was miraculously converted on the way (Acts 9). Saul's conversion was a major turning point, and an example of God using adversity to further His own purposes, as He so often does. From being a persecutor of the churches, he (referred to as Paul the apostle) would become the major founder and builder of churches of God throughout the Gentile part of the Roman Empire. He would have to suffer a great deal personally in doing so. He referred to himself as *"a wise master builder"* (1 Corinthians 3:10).

Staying united while spreading out

Largely through the efforts of a man nicknamed Barnabas, a great many people were *"added to the Lord"* in the city of Antioch, well over two hundred miles north of Galilee (Acts 11:24). It had started with the persecuted disciples arriving there from Jerusalem and spreading the Word. Barnabas went up from Jerusalem to establish a church there. Then he recognized that he needed help in teaching and supporting these new disciples, and so he continued on to Tarsus, which was not far away, and brought back Paul, who had been back there in his home town for several years. It was while Paul and Barnabas were both in Antioch that they were called by the Holy Spirit to engage in enlarging the work (Acts 13:2).

During this time of expansion, we see several instances of how these increasingly spread-out churches stayed united. For example, a prophet visited Antioch from Jerusalem (Acts 21:10). Prophets with direct revelation from God were used in those days to complement the apostles (Ephesians 4:11), as there were as yet no written New Testament Scriptures. Another practical example of their unity was when the saints in Antioch sent relief to their fellow-saints in Jerusalem and Judaea when a famine was imminent (Acts 11:29,30). There was obviously communication between these churches.

Meanwhile in Jerusalem, king Herod Agrippa spearheaded a new wave of the persecution. It cost the apostle James his life. It looked as if Peter would suffer a similar fate, but the church constantly prayed for him (Acts 12:5). From this point on James, the brother of the Lord Jesus, became more prominent in the life of the church in Jerusalem. In fact, it was during this phase that we begin to see the transition from apostles to other elders (Acts 11:30), and the need for there to be elders in each church to care for the saints (Titus 1:5).

Maintaining the churches

The apostle Paul often revisited many of the newly established churches. He knew that they needed follow-up teaching and support. It was not enough to establish them and then leave them on their own. This on-going building up was a vital part of maintaining these churches in the faith as they multiplied and spread out. It was important that they stayed part of the one fellowship, and did not become just independent churches, practicing what each thought best.

Acts chapter 15 describes a landmark event—a gathering of apostles and elders from Jerusalem and Antioch to resolve a question as to the teaching of the Lord about what was required for disciples: whether circumcision was necessary, as it had been under Judaism. Had they not resolved it by consultation, the issue could have caused a severe breach in the young community. It could have led to them no longer being the one fellowship of God's Son. Quite apart from the issue itself, the process they used is particularly enlightening. The apostles were involved because it had been given to them to lay down the foundation teaching; the other elders were involved because they would have the on-going responsibility to care for the churches and safeguard the teaching in the absence of the apostles. From this gathering we get the pattern of elders' meetings as the process for discovering or confirming the teaching of the Lord, so as to maintain unity of teaching and prac-tice throughout the churches of God.

After this conference Paul and his companion Silas travelled back through the churches, informing them of the decision: *"Now while they were passing through the cities, they were delivering the decrees which had been decided upon by the apostles and elders who were in Jerusalem, for them to observe. So the churches were being strengthened in the faith, and were increasing in number daily"* (Acts 16:4,5). They arrived in Jerusalem divided but they returned home united, by which the saints were encouraged and strengthened.

As the New Testament epistles began to be disseminated, the faith was being delivered in writing gradually to the saints. By the time Jude wrote about it in his epistle, the faith had been *"once for all delivered to the saints"* (Jude verse 3). It had not been delivered all at once, but by then it had been delivered completely.

The foundation had been laid and will remain until the end of the age when the Lord returns (Matthew 28:20). These epistles now constitute for us a great written heritage.

The apostles' teaching has never been revoked; it applies every bit as much today. Romans 6:17 expresses it this way:

> *"But thanks be to God that though you were slaves of sin, you became obedient from the heart to that form of teaching to which you were committed."*

This shows that, not only was the teaching delivered to the saints (Jude verse 3), but the saints were delivered to it—to the "form" (the word means a mould or pattern) of teaching to which they were to conform themselves. As each church of God had been planted, it had come out of the same mould of teaching, and this resulted in a network of consistent inter-dependent churches. It was among such churches that the Lord Jesus walked, as Revelation 1 describes. He was able to walk among them as long as they would submit to His authority. The disciples had to be fitted into this divine pattern and teaching; the teaching could not be adapted to their own views or preferences.

The pattern set for us

As we look back over the early history of the churches of God as recorded in the New Testament, we see a number of important trends over the course of those critically important forty or so years:

- It began with about one hundred and twenty people being all assembled with one accord in one place in Jerusalem, but it progressed to being a network of inter-dependent churches throughout dozens of towns and cities in the Roman Empire. They were a community, a fellowship.

- It began being restricted to Jews, the small remnant of Israel who believed in and were committed to follow their Messiah, but it progressed to being a universal, multi-cultural community to which persons of all racial backgrounds and social status were admitted.

- It began with the Word of God being revealed orally by apostles such as Peter and Paul, as well as by prophets such as Judas and Silas (Acts 15:32), and authenticated by miraculous signs. It progressed to a written record of events and teaching, which constituted the New Testament and which, together with the Old Testament, formed the authoritative "canon" (standard) of Scripture.

- It began with the Lord Jesus instructing His apostles after His resurrection to teach *"all that I commanded you"*, which became known as *"the apostles' doctrine"* (teaching), and then as *"the faith once for all delivered to the saints,"* which was the basis of the unity of the community.

• It began with twelve apostles of the Lord Jesus, who had seen Him and received His commandments personally, and progressed to a unique system of governance by a collective elderhood.

It is this last matter of leadership in the churches to which we now need to turn our attention.

16.

Leadership in the Churches

"To all the saints in Christ Jesus who are in Philippi, including the overseers and deacons"
(Philippians 1:1)

The church the Body of Christ has no human leaders. It is a spiritual entity where each member of the Body is directly under the headship of Christ. He is the Head of the Body, and each member has equal status in it: *"There is neither Jew nor Greek, there is neither slave nor free man, there is neither male nor female; for you are all one in Christ Jesus"* (Galatians 3:28). However, from the outset, human leadership was needed (and was provided) in churches of God, with distinct roles.

Apostles

The Lord had given direct responsibility to His eleven apostles before His departure. Then Matthias was added, and later Paul. They were *"apostles of our Lord Jesus Christ"* (Jude verse 17). Peter and Paul both wrote more than once in their epistles that they were "apostles of Jesus Christ," highlighting that it was by His divine appointment. Paul also said, *"Am I not an apostle? ... Have I not seen Jesus Christ our Lord?"* (1 Corinthians 9:1). They carried authority as those who had seen Him and received His commandments personally.

The apostles had particular responsibility in the early days to make the major decisions (such as arranging for the appointment of men in the Jerusalem church to oversee the care of the widows, Acts 6:1–4), and to mentor other elders (e.g. Titus 1:4). The *"apostles teaching"* (Acts 2:42) was to be relayed to others as Paul described in 2 Timothy 2:2, *"The things which you have heard from me in the presence of many witnesses, entrust these to faithful men who will be able to teach others also."* However, once they passed on, no others were appointed to succeed them as apostles.

"Apostolic succession" is not something that is taught in Scripture. The only case of this was Matthias replacing Judas, as described in Acts 1:26, to restore the number of apostles to twelve. In addition, the apostle Paul was specially raised up, as *"one untimely born"* (1 Corinthians 15:8), to take the message to the Gentiles as well as to the Jews (Acts 9:15). [20] And so by the time most of them had died, the work of apostles was done. The foundation teaching had been passed on to the churches in its entirety (Jude verse 3).

The apostles played the pivotal role in the beginning. They were the nucleus around which the kingdom of God was developed after the Lord's departure. They were the ones who were told to go and make disciples, which is how the kingdom was to be populated. Therefore, as disciples were made and baptized, they had to join themselves with those apostles, adhering to their teaching, to be in the kingdom of God. There was to be one flock of God, under one shepherd, even after Gentiles were added (John 10:14).

Elders (also referred to as overseers and bishops)

It was over that flock that overseers were appointed by the Holy Spirit in the churches of God, to care for them as under-shepherds (Acts 20:28,29; 1 Peter 5:2,3). It is Acts 11:30 that we read explicitly about elders in a church of God for the first time. Just as there had been elders in Israel in the Old Testament, men who played an important part in the governance of the people, so elders were appointed to govern and care for churches of God. In fact, the absence of elders in any church was a lack that needed to be remedied, as Paul instructed Titus: *"For this reason I left you in Crete, that you should set in order the things that are lacking, and appoint elders in every city as I commanded you"* (Titus 1:5 NKJV). More than one elder was to be appointed in each place.

Because existing elders were the ones who appointed other elders, specifications were given as to the type of men they should appoint. (These requirements are listed in 1 Timothy 3:2–7 and Titus 1:6–8.) However, as Paul pointed out to the elders of the church in Ephesus when he met with them at Miletus, it is the Holy Spirit who actually appoints them (Acts 20:28,29). It is then men's responsibility to recognize where He has done that and to implement that appointment.

Elders are to work collectively, and the unity of the elderhood is essential both within one assembly and across the entire fellowship of assemblies. Together they must safeguard the teaching of the Lord, *"holding fast the faithful word which is in accordance with the teaching, so that he will be able both to exhort in sound doctrine and to refute those who contradict"* (Titus 1:9). Otherwise the house of God could not continue to have uniform teaching and be *"the pillar and support of the truth"* (1 Timothy 3:15).

---

20 Matthias had been with the Lord (Acts 1:21-23). Paul was given a special revelation by the Lord to equip him for his work (Acts 26:16-18; 1 Corinthians 9:1; 11:23; 15:8).

This unity of the elderhood is the unity of the whole elderhood, not just a subset of it (such as exists in a hierarchy, where some decisions are made "at the top"). Rule is by elders in each church, who consult together to maintain unity of teaching and practice. Decisions of such elders together are binding; otherwise the unity would not be maintained. The application of the decisions is in the local churches, by the local elders, and requires their submission to those collective decisions. United elderhood is a unique and divinely-designed form of rule.

There are several Scriptures addressed to elders, or written about them, that show what their particular responsibilities are:

- The overall leadership and governance of the church.
  "Obey your leaders and submit to them, for they keep watch over your souls as those who will give an account. Let them do this with joy and not with grief, for this would be unprofitable for you" (Hebrews 13:17).

- The spiritual care of the saints.
  "Take care of the church of God" (1 Timothy 3:5). *"Admonish the unruly, encourage the fainthearted, help the weak, be patient with everyone"* (1 Thessalonians 5:14). *"Shepherd the flock of God among you, exercizing oversight ... "* (1 Peter 5:2).

- Teaching the Scriptures.
  "Prescribe and teach these things" (1 Timothy 4:11). *"The things which you have heard from me in the presence of many witnesses, entrust these to faithful men who will be able to teach others also"* (2 Timothy 2:2,3).

- Guarding the doctrine.
  "Reprove, rebuke, exhort, with great patience and instruction" (2 Timothy 4:2). *"Guard what has been entrusted to you"* (1 Timothy 6:20). *"They were delivering the decrees which had been decided upon by the apostles and elders who were in Jerusalem, for them to observe"* (Acts 16:4).

- Recognizing gift, for giving responsibility in the church.
  "Do not neglect the spiritual gift within you, which was bestowed on you through prophetic utterance with the laying on of hands by the presbytery" (1 Timothy 4:14) [21]. *"Set in order the things that are lacking, and appoint elders"* (Titus1:5 NKJV).

---

21 This reference to the laying on of hands by the elders together in 1 Timothy 4:14 was for the purpose of jointly recognizing Timothy's gift and commending him to his sphere of service. The word used for "by" is *"meta"*—meaning that it was "accompanied by" the laying on of hands, not "by means of." This act did not confer any special powers, such as had been the case in Acts 8:18, where the word *"dia"* is used, indicating "by means of."

- Ensuring the care of the needy.
  "To send a contribution for the relief of the brethren living in Judea. This they also did, sending it ... to the elders" (Acts 11:29,30). *"You must help the weak"* (Acts 20:35).

- Resolving conflict in the church.
  "See that no one repays another with evil for evil, but always seek after that which is good for one another and for all people" (1 Thessalonians 5:15).

- Guiding the church in applying discipline, excommunication, and restoration.
  "Those who continue in sin, rebuke in the presence of all, so that the rest also will be fearful of sinning" (1 Timothy 5:20). *"Reject a factious man after a first and second warning"* (Titus 3:10).

- Being role models.
  "Proving to be examples to the flock" (1 Peter 5:3). *"Be on guard for yourselves and for all the flock, among which the Holy Spirit has made you overseers, to shepherd the church of God which He purchased with His own blood"* (Acts 20:28).

Because oversight work is a united work, it requires continual consultation and co-operation, including subjection to one another. 3 John verses 9,10 refer to the case of Diotrephes who was putting people out of the church because they wanted to receive brethren among them, which he was prohibiting. This shows the potential danger of an individual man having the authority. Overseers working together show the uniting effect of the Holy Spirit in what they do.

Matters affecting individual saints concern the overseers in that local church, since they are charged with the care of that church (1 Timothy 3:5). Matters of doctrine and uniform practice need to go to levels of the oversight beyond the local church for agreement (such as occurred in Acts 15). The conference of apostles and elders in Acts 15 sets the pattern for this process. The conclusion on that occasion was expressed as follows: *"It seemed good to the Holy Spirit, and to us"* (Acts 15:28). Afterwards the apostle Paul and Silas (an elder) went around the churches communicating the decision, described as "decrees." The result was the up-building of the churches (Acts 16:5).

The early churches were grouped in districts or regions. We read of the churches in Galatia (1 Corinthians 16:1), Macedonia (2 Corinthians 8:1), Judea (Galatians 1:22), and Asia (Revelation 1:4). Overseers of these districts may well have met as they found it necessary in order to deal with matters of mutual concern. [22] If

---

22 Examples of such joint action are: (a) the commendation of Timothy, a brother to accompany Paul, by the brethren of two assemblies (Acts 16:2), who may well have constituted (or been part of) the "presbytery" (group of elders) who publicly recog-

the fellowship of churches had not been based on united adherence to the apostles' teaching (*"the unity of the faith"* Ephesians 4:13), their inter-dependence and mutual accountability would not have been necessary. They could each have operated on their own. The local overseers would not have needed to pursue unity beyond their own church. But this was not the divine pattern.

The relationship of overseers to the rest of the saints in a church of God is described as being *"among"* them, and a warning is given to them not to abuse their authority:

> *"Shepherd the flock of God among you, exercising oversight not under compulsion, but voluntarily, according to the will of God; and not for sordid gain, but with eagerness; nor yet as lording it over those allotted to your charge, but proving to be examples to the flock. And when the Chief Shepherd appears, you will receive the unfading crown of glory"* (1 Peter 5:2–4).

On the other hand, the saints are accountable to their overseers. They are to respect their overseers' authority and to imitate their faith as seen in their godly lives:

> *"Remember those who led you, who spoke the word of God to you; and considering the result of their conduct, imitate their faith ... Obey your leaders and submit to them, for they keep watch over your souls as those who will give an account. Let them do this with joy and not with grief, for this would be unprofitable for you."* (Hebrews 13:7,17).

The church of God in Thessalonica was told that their overseers were *"over you in the Lord"* (1 Thessalonians 5:12). Here again is the expression "in the Lord" which, as we discovered earlier, refers to those who are gathered in obedience to the Lord in God's churches in the kingdom of God. Obviously, these overseers were not over other believers who were not in the church. There are no overseers or elders over the church the Body of Christ. As we saw previously, the expression "in the Lord" does not automatically apply to all believers in the Body.

Deacons

In addition to overseers, deacons were appointed in the early churches: *"To all the saints in Christ Jesus who are in Philippi, including the overseers and deacons"* (Philippians 1:1). Their qualifications are shown in 1 Timothy 3:8–13.

The word deacon means a servant, and these men were appointed to serve the saints. As we saw earlier, this is a different word (Greek: *"diakonos"*) than the word

---

nized his gift and ministry; and (b) the joint appointment by churches of a brother to travel with the apostle Paul and Titus in their work of delivering a gift from the saints (2 Corinthians 8:18-20).

used for service to God, such as worship (Greek: "*leitourgos*"). Christ is referred to as a minister (servant) in both capacities—towards men and women when He was on Earth, and towards God on our behalf in heaven now:

- "*The Son of Man did not come to be served, but to serve* ['diakonos'], *and to give His life a ransom for many*" (Matthew 20:28).

- "*We have such a high priest ... a minister* ['leitourgos'] *in the sanctuary ... He has obtained a more excellent ministry*" (Hebrews 8:1,2,6).

All men and women in a church of God have an opportunity to be servants of the church. For example, the woman Phoebe and the man Tychicus are both described in this way (Romans 16:1; Ephesians 6:21). However, it appears that only men were recognized in this position, where it was their on-going responsibility. In 1 Timothy 3:8, it is explicit that those who are recognized as deacons should be men and, since this is a leadership position, it is consistent with the limitations given in 1 Timothy 2:12 regarding the role of women in the church. [23]

Pastors

Many Christian churches today have one or more ordained pastors, often professionally trained and qualified. They often undertake much of the service of the church, with the congregation sometimes being a relatively passive audience. However, all saints in the churches of God are part of the priesthood and should be active in its service. There is no distinction given in Scripture between a clergy and a congregation.

In the New Testament churches of God, the responsibility of pastoring (caring for) the saints belonged to the overseers. As pastors ("shepherds") they were accountable to the Lord Jesus as the Chief Shepherd: "*I exhort the elders among you ... shepherd the flock of God among you ... when the Chief Shepherd appears, you will receive the unfading crown of glory*" (1 Peter 5:1–4).

---

23 This has nothing to do with inherent superiority or inferiority, but with God's prescribed order.

17.

Building Up the Churches

"I laid a foundation, and another is building on it. But each man must be careful how he builds on it."
(1 Corinthians 3:10)

God is a builder of churches, and He uses men and women to do the building. We therefore can have the privilege of building something of permanent value for God. And if we do, we will be rewarded for it: *"Each man's work will become evident; for the day will show it because it is to be revealed with fire, and the fire itself will test the quality of each man's work. If any man's work which he has built on it remains, he will receive a reward"* (1 Corinthians 3:13,14). The honour however goes to the builder, who is God (Hebrews 3:3,4).

God builds His house in three directions at once—"on," "together," and "up." Let's look at each of these.

Building on

"Having been built on the foundation of the apostles and prophets, Christ Jesus Himself being the corner stone" (Ephesians 2:20).

Firstly, for it to be a church of God, a church must be built *on* the right foundation, which is the teaching of the Lord Jesus Christ, as we have seen. The apostle Paul said to the church at Corinth, *"I laid a foundation, and another is building on it. But each man must be careful how he builds on it. For no man can lay a foundation other than the one which is laid, which is Jesus Christ. Now if anyone builds on the foundation with gold, silver, precious stones, wood, hay, straw, each man's work will become evident ..."* (1 Corinthians 3:10–13).

Like the first one in Jerusalem, therefore, a church of God must be built based on what the apostles originally taught, which is the entire body of teaching that they received from the Lord. Any church that is not based on this full teaching of Christ as given to His apostles cannot be a church of God, and therefore cannot be part of the house of God, which is the pillar and support of the truth (1

Timothy 3:15). God only gives His name to what He originates. This teaching corresponds to the first element that the church in Jerusalem devoted themselves to, as listed in Acts 2:42. (Appendix B identifies some key elements of this foundational teaching, which came to be referred to as "the faith.")

Building together

"In whom the whole building, being fitted together, is growing into a holy temple in the Lord" (Ephesians 2:21).

Secondly, a church of God must be built together with other churches of God to form a united community. This is *"the unity of the faith"* that Paul wrote about (Ephesians 4:13). It is not enough that a church of Christians be doing the right things; it must also be connected to the others. It must be part of the one community. This corresponds to the second item in Acts 2:42—"the fellowship." God's purposes are collective, and He desires unity among His people.

It must have been difficult for those early churches to stay united in doctrine and fellowship in the first century. They did not have the means of travel and communications that we have, and they were constantly facing opposition. As mentioned previously, they used several means, that apply similarly to us today:

- Consistent oral teaching in all the churches (Acts 20:2). The apostle Paul told the Corinthians that he ordained the same things in every church (1 Corinthians 7:17).

- Letters (epistles) sent, read, and circulated among the churches, constituting a body of authoritative Christian literature (Colossians 4:16).

- Visits to the churches, and saints being commended from one to another for full fellowship (Acts 18:27; Romans 16:1).

- Prayer for saints in all the churches. The apostle Paul often wrote that he was praying for the saints in the churches; they were his greatest concern (Colossians 1:3; 2 Corinthians 11:28).

- Relief to meet financial need in other churches (Acts 11:29,30). Good works were important (Galatians 2:10), and their first priority was to be those of "the household of the faith" (Galatians 6:10).

- Support for the spread of the gospel in other places. Paul praised the Philippians for their participation in the gospel (Philippians 1:5). In addition to preaching it locally themselves, they were praying for his work and were supporting it financially.

- Unity of oversight, by consulting with each other about matters which could otherwise divide them, to learn the mind of the Spirit (Acts 15:28).

There are many references in the epistles to this maintenance of unity, especially in the writings of the apostle Paul, who travelled widely among the churches:

- *"just as I teach everywhere in every church"* (1 Corinthians 4:17);
- *"so I direct in all the churches"* (1 Corinthians 7:17);
- *"we have no other practice, nor have the churches of God"* (1 Corinthians 11:16);
- *"as in all the churches of the saints"* (1 Corinthians 14:33);
- *"through all the churches"* (2 Corinthians 8:18);
- *"the daily pressure on me of concern for all the churches"* (2 Corinthians 11:28);
- *"have it also read in the church of the Laodiceans"* (Colossians 4:16);
- *"you … became imitators of the churches of God in Christ Jesus that are in Judea"* (1 Thessalonians 2:14); and
- *"what the Spirit says to the churches"* (Revelation 2:7,11,17, 29; 3:6,13,22).

Building up

"You also, as living stones, are being built up as a spiritual house" (1 Peter 2:5).

Thirdly, a church of God must be being built up through spiritual life and service. A church that does not gather regularly for the breaking of bread or for the prayers, for example (the third and fourth items in Acts 2:42), cannot be a church of God. A church that specializes in only some selected aspect of the service of God but does not engage in the others cannot be a church of God.

In addition, a church of God can become spiritually dead (although that description may not apply to every saint in it). The Lord Jesus warned the church in Sardis:

"I know your deeds, that you have a name that you are alive, but you are dead. Wake up, and strengthen the things that remain, which were about to die; for I have not found your deeds completed in the sight of My God. So remember what you have received and heard; and keep it, and repent" (Revelation 3:1-3).

Similarly, He warned the church in Ephesus:

"I have this against you, that you have left your first love. Therefore remember from where you have fallen, and repent and do the deeds you did at first; or else I am coming to you and will remove your lampstand out of its place—unless you repent. Yet this you do have, that you hate the deeds of the Nicolaitans, which I also hate" (Revelation 2:4–6).

He was saying that, unless they responded and changed, they would no longer be recognized by God, even if they continued to meet and carry out certain activity.

In effect these three aspects of God's building work define what is a church of God. They are the criteria whereby we can assess whether a gathering of baptized disciples is in fact a "church of God":

- Is it built ON the full teaching of the Lord Jesus Christ, as passed on by the apostles, and recorded in the New Testament? and

- Is it built TOGETHER to be united in teaching and operation with other churches of God as the fellowship of God's Son? and

- Is it built UP through authentic spiritual activity and service?

Spiritual gifts

The work of edifying (spiritually building up) a church is carried out by the saints in it exercising their God-given spiritual gifts: *"There are varieties of gifts, but the same Spirit. And there are varieties of ministries, and the same Lord. There are varieties of effects, but the same God who works all things in all persons. But to each one is given the manifestation of the Spirit for the common good"* (1 Corinthians 12:4–7).

From this passage of Scripture we can see three things that are linked together, involving all three persons of the godhead:

- our ministries (service) for the Lord;

- our gifts from the Holy Spirit to enable us to carry out those ministries; and

- the activities and arrangements in which they are carried out, as co-ordinated by God.

The gifts are given by the Spirit to all members of the Body, and given for the benefit of us all.

Romans 12:6–8 and 1 Corinthians 12:4–11 are two Scriptures in particular that list a number of such gifts. A fully-functioning church of God gives ample scope for the exercise of various gifts by the saints in it. The church in Corinth was described by the apostle as coming short in no gift (1 Corinthians 1:7). The particular emphasis in service that any one church is able to give is largely determined by the gifts that those in it have been provided with. The gifts are intended to be used in harmony with each other for the strengthening of the church and its work.

However service that is directed towards God, rather than to each other, is not a matter of specialized gift. Worship and prayer are for all to engage in. They are not restricted to certain saints.

The distinct roles of men and women

In the Body of Christ there is no gender distinction—*"no male or female"* (Galatians 3:28). However in a church of God there are male and female distinctions. The apostle Paul wrote to the church at Corinth about being God's sons and daughters (2 Corinthians 6:16-18). And he said to them, *"I want you to understand that Christ is the head of every man, and the man is the head of a woman, and God is the head of Christ"* (1 Corinthians 11:3). There is a clear order here—from God to Christ, to man, to woman. In each pairing, the relationship is characterized by one being the head and the other showing subjection, all to the glory of God.

Christ Himself was the perfect example of this. His entire ministry on Earth was for the purpose of glorifying His Father. Similarly, it is the man's role to glorify Christ (and in so doing to glorify God), and the woman's to glorify the man (1 Corinthians 11:7). However, there is also inter-dependency (1 Corinthians 11:11). A woman is given hair as her glory, but in her role in the church she is to cover it. In showing subjection to the man in a church setting, a woman is in effect showing it to Christ and to God when the assembly is together in divine order. Similarly, by showing His subjection to Christ, a man also shows it to God. [24]

This distinction in roles in the service of the church is to be demonstrated in several distinct ways, the apostle stated. These are summarized as follows:

---

24 This church situation is distinct from a marriage relationship, for example, where there are also distinct roles of headship and subjection between husbands and wives, which Paul deals with in Ephesians 5:22–33.

Men	Women
HEAD COVERING (1 Corinthians 11:4–16)	
Their heads are to remain uncovered while they are speaking, either to God or a message from God; they thereby show their distinction from the women.	Their heads are to be covered in these situations. Their head covering is worn as a sign that they are under authority.
SPEAKING WHEN THE CHURCH IS GATHERED AS A CHURCH (1 Corinthians 11:18; 14:34; 1 Timothy 2:8)	
Men are the ones to participate audibly in the church gatherings by speaking on behalf of the assembly in worship and prayer, and in speaking to the assembly.	The women remain silent (do not speak out individually) in these gatherings, although they join in the collective singing and saying the "Amen."
POSITIONS OF AUTHORITY (1 Corinthians 14:26,34; 1 Timothy 2:8)	
Men are the ones to teach and lead. Elders and deacons are to be men.	The women are not to teach or have authority over the men.

Some of these requirements are quite different from what many societies today consider appropriate. However, they represent God's prescription for conduct in His kingdom, and they have great significance. They should not be dismissed as having only cultural relevance in the first century.

Behaviour and discipline

Whether we focus on our relationship to God in the churches of God, in the house of God, or in the kingdom of God, a consistent theme emerges from Scripture—holiness and godly behaviour is expected: *"Holiness befits Your house, O Lord, forevermore"* (Psalm 93:5). There are consequences if we live otherwise. We are told to put to death the fleshly nature in us that leads to sin (Galatians 5:24). We are also told that, when we sin, we are to confess that sin to God (1 John 1:9); we are then given the promise that God will unconditionally forgive us and cleanse us from all unrighteousness.

When a problem exists between two people in the church, the process is given to us for dealing with it. In giving this instruction, the Lord dealt with two related situations:

- Where one person has a difficulty with someone else in the church:
  "If your brother sins, go and show him his fault in private; if he listens to you, you have won your brother. But if he does not listen to you, take one or two more with you, so that by the mouth of two or three witnesses every fact may be confirmed. If he refuses to listen to them, tell it to the church; and if he refuses to listen even to the church, let him be to you as a Gentile and a tax collector" (Matthew 18:15–17); and

- Where someone knows that another person has difficulty with them:
  "If you are presenting your offering at the altar, and there remember that your brother has something against you, leave your offering there before the altar and go; first be reconciled to your brother, and then come and present your offering" (Matthew 5:23,24).

In both cases, it is imperative that the matter be dealt with, and dealt with promptly. In the Matthew 18 case, it explicitly says that the situation could become serious enough to warrant excommunication from the church—*"let him be to you as a Gentile and a tax collector."*

Sin by a brother or sister in a church taints that church, and the church has a responsibility to address it. The apostle Paul compared sin in an assembly to leaven (yeast) that spreads to others. Sin can contaminate those around it. The church in Corinth was told to purge out the sin in it (1 Corinthians 5:6,7). This chapter addresses a particular case of immorality in a church, and the apostle Paul was very explicit about how the saints were to deal with it. He said: *"Put away from yourselves the evil person"* (1 Corinthians 5:13). He was instructing the church to excommunicate the man, to put him out of the church, *"for the destruction of the flesh"* (verse 5). It would appear from 2 Corinthians chapter 2, verse 7 that the man later repented and was restored to the church.

1 Corinthians 5:11 lists sins for which excommunication applies. There are similar lists of serious sins in 1 Corinthians 6:9,10; Galatians 5:19–21, and Ephesians 5:5, where the consequence of a person being excommunicated is described as them losing their inheritance in the kingdom of God.

If sin is not dealt with in a church of God it may incur the judgment of God. For example, the Lord said to the church in Thyatira:

"You tolerate the woman Jezebel, who calls herself a prophetess, and she teaches and leads My bond-servants astray so that they commit acts of immorality and eat things sacrificed to idols. I gave her time to repent, and she does not want

to repent of her immorality. Behold, I will throw her on a bed of sickness, and those who commit adultery with her into great tribulation, unless they repent of her deeds. And I will kill her children with pestilence, and all the churches will know that I am He who searches the minds and hearts; and I will give to each one of you according to your deeds" (Revelation 2:20–23).

He was protecting the holiness of His house.

Edification

The apostle Paul was continually engaged in the building up (edifying) of what God was building in each place. He wrote to the church at Colosse: *"As you have received Christ Jesus the Lord, so walk in Him, having been firmly rooted and now being built up in Him and established in your faith, just as you were instructed, and overflowing with gratitude"* (Colossians 2:6,7). The churches were a pre-occupation with him, as he admitted: *"There is the daily pressure on me of concern for all the churches"* (2 Corinthians 11:28).

Churches of God are intended to provide support for the disciples in them, providing care, fellowship, encouragement, and opportunity for service. This is what God looks for in His churches, and it is how the saints in them show their love to Him. We are not expected to live our Christian lives alone.

Many church organizations in the world today are highly specialized. They focus on one or two important aspects of the work of God, such as missions, charitable activity, or preaching the Word. However, a scriptural church of God is intended to be a full-scope church, exhibiting all aspects of the life and service of disciples. Thus we should expect to see it regularly engaged in

- Worship;
- Prayer;
- Making (and baptizing and adding) disciples;
- Teaching the Word of God;
- Supporting and caring for each other;
- Doing good to others outside the church; and
- Enjoying fellowship with each other.

All of this, of course, must be more than just activity. It must be soundly based on genuine devotion to the Lord Jesus.

18.

Making the Connections

"You are Christ's body"; "you are a temple of God"; "He has made us to be a kingdom"
(1 Corinthians 12:27; 1 Corinthians 3:16; Revelation 1:6)

As we discover the truth of churches of God from Scripture—that is, how disciples ought to gather to serve the Lord in these days—we will realize that it is not an isolated truth. While it is confined to the present period from Pentecost to the Lord's return, it is all part of an integrated pattern that reflects the very character of God. This truth about God's church is distinct from, and yet connected to, the spiritual realities of (a) the church the Body of Christ, (b) the house of God, and (c) the kingdom of God.

Connected to the Body of Christ

The question might be asked: Since a church of God does not simply consist of local members of the Body of Christ who gather together, what is the connection between the churches of God and the church the Body of Christ? Both of them have the name "church," meaning people called out to be together by God. Why then does He call out two churches?

Paul wrote to the church of God in Corinth, *"You are Christ's body"* (1 Corinthians 12:27) (not "you are *'the'* body of Christ," because they were only part of it). Each disciple in the church at Corinth was also a member of that Body, and so he told them they were not to act independently of one another. He wrote this in the context of them using their various spiritual gifts, which they had each received from the Holy Spirit. Each gift was to be used in the church at Corinth in conjunction with each other's, without regarding one as more important than the other. What was important was the overall effect. The over-riding purpose of these gifts was not just that each person would feel fulfilled, but that all the saints would be built up (Ephesians 4:12, 16). The apostle said to the church in Corinth, *"Since you are zealous of spiritual gifts, seek to abound for the edification of the church"* (1 Corinthians 14:12).

The Body of Christ is a spiritual union that pertains to the perfect relationship that exists among believers, and between them and their Head, who is Christ. It focuses on the inter-relationships and inter-dependencies of those believers. God intends that all members of Christ's Body on Earth be in churches of God to obediently live and serve there together, in full accordance with the Lord's commands and in full harmony with each other. In fact the only legitimate way that full unity of living members of the Body can be exhibited in practice is in scriptural churches of God. And so God calls disciples into His churches as the place where they can primarily function in relation to others.

For someone to say that membership in the Body of Christ is all that is required to be in a scriptural church of God is to ignore the clear teaching of Scripture about the need for baptism, addition, and continuing steadfastly as the church in Jerusalem did. The "Great Commission" from the Lord Jesus included teaching disciples to do "*all*" that He commanded (Matthew 28:18–20). This is not just a nice ideal but a prerequisite for serving God acceptably.

When Paul addressed the saints in the churches of God in both Ephesus and Colosse, he described them as those who were "faithful in Christ." They were not only believers in Christ; they were being faithful as His disciples, which is what kept them together as the church of God.

God's call is into both the Body of Christ and churches of God; they are quite distinct things. The former is perfect, seated in the heavenly places [25] in Christ (Ephesians 2:6). Nothing can spoil that relationship in any way. It is not affected by sin or disobedience. There are no conditions to remaining in it. However, the opposite is true for churches of God. They are gatherings for service and obedience. There are requirements to be met in order to be added to them, and requirements in order to remain in them. It is our human limitations and weaknesses, not God's design, that prevents us all as believers being in churches that are "churches of God." Christ is building the church which is His Body unconditionally for Himself, and it will continue in union with Him eternally. But the churches of God are a divine arrangement for the present period of time, so that God may be served acceptably in the interval until Christ returns.

Connected to the house of God

As we saw in the last section, the house of God is where God dwells on Earth among His people, who have separated themselves to Him (1 Corinthians 3:16; 2

---

25   "The heavenlies" (Greek: '*epouranios*') (Ephesians 1:3, 20; 2:6; 3:10; 6:12) is to be distinguished from "the holy place" in the immediate presence of God (Hebrews 9:8, 12, 24; 10:19), which is discussed in chapter 6 and elsewhere.

Corinthians 6:16–18). It is the pillar and support of the truth of God (1 Timothy 3:15). It is where disciples are being built up together to worship and serve God (1 Peter 2:5,9). As we have seen in this section, the churches of God are where God intends disciples to gather to serve Him. And so Scripture closely links the house of God with the churches of God.

We see this in 1 Timothy 3:5,15 where taking care of a church of God is described as being part of the conduct expected in the house of God: *"If a man does not know how to manage his own household, how will he take care of the church of God? … I write so that you will know how one ought to conduct himself in the household of God, which is the church of the living God, the pillar and support of the truth."*

We see it also in Ephesians 2:21,22 where the church in Ephesus is described as being part of the holy temple that God is building: *"In whom the whole building, being fitted together, is growing into a holy temple in the Lord, in whom you also are being built together into a dwelling of God in the Spirit."*

In addition, we see it in the linkage of the spiritual worship of those in the house of God with their gathering themselves together in Hebrews 10:25: *"Since we have a great priest over the house of God, let us draw near with a sincere heart in full assurance of faith … and let us consider how to stimulate one another to love and good deeds, not forsaking our own assembling together …"*

We see it again in 1 Corinthians 3:16 where the church of God in Corinth was told: *"Do you not know that you are [a] temple of God and that the Spirit of God dwells in you?"*

And so Scripture teaches that it is those disciples gathered in churches of God that form God's house on Earth today, as a collective entity.

Connected to the kingdom of God

The kingdom of God is the community on Earth where Christ's authority is collectively acknowledged and carried out (Matthew 6:10). The kingdom was given to Israel in the past (Exodus 19:6), but they eventually lost it due to their unfaithfulness and disobedience. It was then transferred to the apostles and other disciples gathered with them, as Christ told them, *"Do not be afraid, little flock, for your Father has chosen gladly to give you the kingdom"* (Luke 12:32). Subsequently the kingdom also included others who were added to them (Acts 8:12; 14:22; 19:8), as "the flock of God" (1 Peter 5:2). It is therefore a place for disciples, believers who genuinely wish to be obedient to Him in unity. The governing law of the kingdom is "the faith", which is what the apostles taught (Acts 14:22).

It was concerning the kingdom of God that the Lord Jesus gave instructions to his apostles before his departure (Acts 1:1-6), and that caused them to establish churches of God wherever they went. It was what the apostle Paul devoted himself to: *"He stayed two full years in his own rented quarters and was welcoming all who came to him, preaching the kingdom of God and teaching concerning the Lord Jesus Christ with all openness, unhindered"* (Acts 28:30,31).

For example, when Paul and Barnabas were travelling in Asia Minor, they returned to revisit three churches—in Lystra, Iconium, and Antioch. It says that while they were there they were:

> *"... strengthening the souls of the disciples, encouraging them to continue in the faith, and saying, 'Through many tribulations we must enter the kingdom of God.' When they had appointed elders for them in every church, having prayed with fasting, they commended them to the Lord in whom they had believed"* (Acts 14:22,23).

Here we see the close connection between the disciples in the local churches of God, with their governing elders, adhering to the faith as the teaching of the Lord that bound them together, all in the kingdom of God.

We further see the connection between the churches and the kingdom (and priesthood) in Revelation 1:4–6: *"John to the seven churches that are in Asia ... He has made us to be a kingdom, priests to His God and Father."*

And so, once again, it becomes clear that those who are gathered in churches of God constitute the kingdom of God on Earth, as one united community.

The same people

There is a pattern therefore, not of disparate groups or entities, but of the same obedient company of people, called together by God to reflect various aspects of His work and relationships with them. All believers are made living stones, sons (and daughters) of God, and are given a birth-right to priesthood at their new birth, when they confess the Son of God as their Saviour and Lord. They have been sanctified (set apart) for those purposes. The privileges of being the house of God, the kingdom of God, the holy and royal priesthood, the holy nation, and the people of God are spiritual realities made possible by the work of Christ. But they must be reflected on Earth by believers' obedience in accordance with God's order.

The living stones must come to be built up in conjunction with the corner stone in order to be a house for God; that is the purpose of living stones. The priests have to function together in it as the priesthood under the great high priest; priests do not just function individually. Disciples are to be joined together in a community of churches, as the kingdom of God, under God's rule. And His sons and daughters have to separate themselves to God to allow Him to regard them as His people (2 Corinthians 6:16-18). This is the divine ideal, and it should be what we as members of the Body of Christ long for also, that all living believers in Christ would constitute these entities on Earth.

Who are included?

The epistles were written to saints gathered together in churches of God. It is in these epistles where we are given the teaching of the house of God, the kingdom of God and other related matters, because it pertained to them. For example, it was to saints in these churches in various places, who had been baptized (1 Peter 3:21) and who were under elders (1 Peter 5:1–3), that the apostle Peter wrote that they were being built up as a spiritual house, that they were a holy priesthood and a royal priesthood (the same priesthood but in different aspects), and that they were a holy nation (1 Peter 2:5,9). He described them as having been chosen to obey Jesus Christ. It was the faithful saints in the church at Ephesus that the apostle Paul described as having been built on the foundation of the apostles and prophets, being fitly framed together to be the temple of God, and being a habitation of God in the Spirit (Ephesians 2:20–22). It was to the saints in the church of God in Corinth that Paul wrote that they were part of the temple (house) of God, and that this required them to be separate from ungodly associations (1 Corinthians 3:16; 2 Corinthians 6:16-18). It was to those who were under overseers that the writer of Hebrews said were the house of God (Hebrews 3:6; 13:17), and that they were receiving the kingdom of God (Hebrews 12:28) [26].

Nowhere does it indicate that any believer not gathered in churches of God was in the temple, or the house, or the kingdom of God.

Important distinctions

And so there are important connections between these various terms that we have been looking at. Three of them—all containing the expression "of God"—refer to the same people, but describe a different aspect of their relationship with Him:

- The church (and churches) of God, focusing on disciples being gathered together in particular places for service and testimony in response to the call of God.

---

26 Those in the church in Corinth were also told that they were members of the Body of Christ (1 Corinthians 12:27); but they were also told that this was due to them having been baptized in the Holy Spirit (1 Corinthians 12:13) and so it applies to all who come in faith to Christ.

- The house of God, focusing on God living among these people, receiving their priestly service.

- The kingdom of God, focusing on their collective subjection to the rule and authority of God, and their resulting conduct.

Aspirations or conditions?

As we saw in chapter 1, our on-going obedience as disciples of the Lord Jesus does not affect our membership in the church the Body of Christ. But, as we have been discovering, this is not true for each of these other relationships. For example:

- Churches of God: Since they are to be a testimony to God in each place where they are located, disciples must be added to them, continue in obedience as they are taught, and maintain their standard of holiness. Sin must be dealt with, and saints may have to be put away from them (1 Corinthians 5:11). It is even possible for an entire church to cease to exist for God (Revelation 2:5).

- The house of God: Since it is to be a holy priesthood, drawing near and offering spiritual sacrifices, making confession to God's name, those in it must continue faithfully and sincerely to exercise the privilege of doing so (Hebrews 3:6). It must stand for and testify to the truth of God (1 Timothy 3:15).

- The kingdom of God: Since it is the place where the rule of God is obeyed, and His righteousness is exhibited, those in it must live righteous lives. The unrighteous are disqualified from having a part in it (1 Corinthians 6:10; Galatians 5:21; Ephesians 5:5).

These conditions are not set forth in Scripture merely as aspirations for those who are in the churches, the house, and the kingdom, but rather as on-going conditions.

In all these cases, continued faithfulness is required. Willful disobedience, ungodly living, disregard of God's truth, or refusal to take advantage of the spiritual privileges that Christ has obtained for us can cause us to forfeit or miss the privileges of these relationships during our lifetimes. Clearly these three things that are "of God" cannot be synonymous with the church that is Christ's Body.

On the other hand, God is extremely compassionate towards honest weakness and failings. We are not expected to have perfect understanding or to achieve sinlessness (1 John 1:8). Provision is made for our ignorance and failure. Nothing is expected of us that we cannot do (2 Corinthians 8:12). But willful disregard of the things of God is quite a different matter: "*God is opposed to the proud, but gives grace to the humble.*" (1 Peter 5:5)

It is important that we understand the distinctions between these expressions, so that we do not assume that as believers we are automatically included in all of these things. The major point, however, is that God desires that all living members of the Body of Christ in fact be part of the churches of God, the house of God, and the kingdom of God, and aim to show in practice the character of the church the Body of Christ in their lives together. That is the ideal to which we as believers in the Lord Jesus should aspire.

19.

God's Church—A Summary

Following is a summary of the main points that we have seen in this section as we have explored the subject of God's church and churches:

- Gathering together in churches is important for disciples. We are not intended merely to serve God alone as individuals.

- It is not left to us to choose where or how to gather. God has prescribed what His church is, and He calls disciples into it through His Word.

- Local churches in the New Testament were referred to as "churches of God." To be a church of God, a church must (a) be built on the foundation teaching of the apostles, (b) be built together in full fellowship with other churches of God, and (c) be built up in spiritual life and service.

- The churches of God are not the same as the Body of Christ, which consists of all believers in Christ from Pentecost until His return to the air. A member of that Body can never cease to be so, regardless of their spiritual condition. However, being in a church of God requires being added to it, and then staying in it.

- The first church of God in Jerusalem set a pattern for us today. It began with disciples being saved, then baptized, and then added, and then continuing in the apostles' teaching, the fellowship, the breaking of bread and the prayers.

- As more churches came into existence, they were formed on the same basis, and they maintained a unity of teaching and practice. They continued as one community.

- Leadership in the churches was initially exercised by the apostles, then passed to other elders who were not apostles, who acted collectively. They were supported by deacons. The elders had the responsibility for the pastoral care of the saints. Unity among the entire elderhood was necessary in order to maintain the common teaching and practice of the community.

- Spiritual gifts have been given to all believers. In the local churches, they are to be used in harmony to strengthen spiritually the saints in them, as well as to make other disciples and to do good to others.

- Within the churches there are distinct roles for men and women, and God's order puts some restrictions on the activities of women.

- Godly living and faithful service is expected of saints in churches of God. Sin by someone in a church taints the church and must be dealt with even, where necessary, to the extent of putting the person away. The eventual aim of such discipline, however, is their subsequent restoration.

Discovering True Worship

How We Can Offer to God What He Really Wants

"Worship God" (the angel in Revelation 22:9)

20.

Why Should We Worship?

"Such people the Father seeks to be His worshipers." (John 4:23)

There is something that God cannot give to Himself. Although He is unlimited in His power and ability and provides everything we need (Acts 17:25), He can only receive that one thing from those He has created. And it is what He longs for from us. It is a primary reason why He made us. It is the one thing that should never be given to anyone or anything other than God. That one thing is worship.

How do people worship?

There is almost an unlimited number of ways that people in this world engage in worship and religious service these days. For example, Buddhists use an image of Buddha and chant mantras. Muslims recite the Koran and pray to Allah five times a day. Native Americans worship nature, both in the sky and on the Earth. Devout orthodox Jews pray with a swaying motion while wearing a yarmulke on their heads. Catholic Christians worship the Virgin Mary, use relics, and celebrate the Mass. Some Protestant churches have a highly formal liturgy and rituals, while others are very emotional and demonstrative. Some Christian services are very traditional, while others are contemporary. Some use worship leaders and performers. Some have special robes and vestments. Some use prescribed books of worship, while others are spontaneous. Some offer worship services for seekers; others just offer them for the members of the congregation. There is an almost endless variety of what is called worship.

Are these all just cultural differences, matters of personal preference or tradition? Does God enjoy this variety? Does it matter to Him how we do it? Is He looking for creativity in how we worship Him? If it does matter how we do it, what kind of worship pleases Him? How can we know whether or not our worship is acceptable to Him? Again we have to turn to God's Word—the Word of truth—for the answers.

Is all worship acceptable?

God cannot possibly regard many of these activities that are listed above as worship of Him (see John 4:22). Worship involves people who know God offering to Him something that He values. The first time the Bible uses the word is in Genesis 22:5 where Abraham, at the mountain in Moriah, *"said to his young men, 'Stay here with the donkey, and I and the lad will go over there; and we will worship and return to you.'"* Abraham was prepared to offer his own son as an act of devotion to God, and it illustrates what God the Father would Himself do years later in offering His own Son at Calvary. It illustrates the essence of what pleases God in worship—appreciation of Christ His Son.

The first people mentioned in history who made offerings to God were Cain and Abel, the two sons of Adam and Eve (Genesis 4:4,5). One of those offerings was accepted and one was not. Presumably Cain and Abel had both been instructed by their parents on how to offer to God, and so it was not just a matter of chance. But Cain did it his own way, by bringing an offering that did not cost a life and was the product of his own labour, and it was not accepted. Abel on the other hand sacrificed a lamb, the best of his flock. This was accepted. And so, right from the start, we see that not all worship is acceptable to God.

Worship is not about us, what we want or what we can do. It is not even primarily about what God has done for us. It is all about God Himself and what He does. The word "worship" comes from the word "worth." Worship of God focuses on His worth and our appreciation of that. Therefore, when we are worshipping, we have to take the focus off ourselves and put it on Him. David, who understood worship very well, put it this way: *"I call upon the LORD, who is worthy to be praised"* (2 Samuel 22:4).

That is the point—God is uniquely worthy to be praised, and that is the fundamental reason for our worship. Therefore, the more we understand Him and His intrinsic worth, and the better we appreciate what He does and has done, the fuller our worship will be.

God wants our worship. He deserves it! And He will get worship—if not from us, then from others. When God's people Israel, at the end of the Old Testament period, was bringing worship to Him that was not acceptable, He said to them: *"'I am not pleased with you,' says the LORD of hosts, 'nor will I accept an offering from you. For from the rising of the sun even to its setting, My name will be great among the nations, and in every place incense is going to be offered to My name, and a grain offering that is pure; for My name will be great among the nations,' says the LORD of hosts"* (Malachi 1:10,11). And then, when the Jewish leaders told Jesus to stop His disciples from praising Him, He replied, *"I tell you, if these become silent, the stones will cry out!"* (Luke 19:40)

Two aspects of worship

When the magi came to see the young child Jesus, the Bible says that *"they fell to the ground and worshiped Him"* (Matthew 2:11). This illustrates two aspects of worship—bowing down in humility before a superior being (paying homage), and then offering up a gift to him. In our worship we bow down our hearts in reverence to God. (The Greek word used is *"proskuneo,"* usually translated "worshipped.") We also offer spiritual sacrifices; this is often referred to as "serving" God (Hebrews 9:14; 12:28).

What is true worship?

When Jesus met the woman of Samaria at Sychar's well, He gave her a wonderful revelation about worship. She had said to Him, *"Our fathers worshiped in this mountain, and you people say that in Jerusalem is the place where men ought to worship."* He then replied to her with this amazing statement:

> *"Woman, believe Me, an hour is coming when neither in this mountain nor in Jerusalem will you worship the Father. You worship what you do not know; we worship what we know, for salvation is from the Jews. But an hour is coming, and now is, when the true worshipers will worship the Father in spirit and truth; for such people the Father seeks to be His worshipers. God is spirit, and those who worship Him must worship in spirit and truth"* (John 4:20–24).

Christ was disclosing to this woman that worship was no longer going to take place at any particular geographic location on Earth, with "earthly ordinances" (Hebrews 9:10), rituals and animal sacrifices (as it had done up to that point, most recently by Jews at the temple in Jerusalem). These were only temporary symbols, which pointed to the real thing that was to come. But now God was about to institute true worship of a spiritual nature, which would come from peoples' hearts, by means of the working of the Holy Spirit of God within them (Philippians 3:3). Jesus told her that this was what God was looking for—to be worshipped *"in spirit and truth"*—that is, in reality. He was looking for "true worshippers."

21.

What Does Worship Involve?

"A holy priesthood, to offer up spiritual sacrifices acceptable to God through Jesus Christ."
(1 Peter 2:5)

When Christ spoke to the woman at the well in John chapter 4, He was introducing the fact that true worship does not involve the presence of God coming down to a place on this Earth (as it did in the tabernacle and temple in the Old Testament), but involves us accessing the presence of God in heaven in our spirits, as we looked at previously. We have been given a spiritual nature as part of our human make-up which enables this to take place. In our worship we *"draw near"* (come close) (Hebrews 10:22) to Him through our spirits. Before we explore what this involves, let's be sure about what it does not involve.

What is not worship?

Some people find certain types of traditional worship services boring. Perhaps there is no band (or not a good one) or no entertainment. Perhaps the service is too quiet, and there is not a dynamic sermon. What is it that they may be looking for that causes them to be disappointed?

Worship is not for audiences; it is for participants. We are not there primarily to receive, but to give to God. Hebrews chapter 10 tells us that, as we draw near in the presence of God, we must do so *"in full assurance of faith"* (verse 22)—that is, fully believing. We need to be conscious of what we are doing spiritually. If we do not come this way, not only will our worship be ineffective, but we may find it deadly dull. But when we do it in full assurance of faith, realizing the reality of the experience, it will become the highlight of our week. We will realize that we have actually been in the presence of God.

Some people prefer a good sermon to participative worship. But hearing the Word spoken to us is intended for our benefit, while worship is for God. Some people prefer just to do work for God; it makes them feel more useful. But God says that He is not worshipped by men's hands as though He needed anything

(Acts 17:25). He is worshipped by us expressing to Him what is in our hearts. That is what He wants to receive from us.

Old Testament worship

People in Old Testament times never had the privilege that we have today of worshipping in spirit and truth in heaven itself. Their access to God was limited, and their consciences were never finally cleansed of their sin, because the animal sacrifices they offered were incapable of getting rid of sin. Sin is always the barrier that keeps us from God.

Israel gathered as the people of God on the designated feast days in the courts of the temple: *"Enter His gates with thanksgiving and His courts with praise"* (Psalm 100:4). Some of the Psalms in our Bible are from those times. They are "songs of ascents"—the "going-up" songs. The city of Jerusalem is at a very high elevation. It is over 2500 feet above sea level and 3700 feet above the Dead Sea, which is only eighteen miles to the east. As the people came on those feast days, from all over the country and lands beyond, they climbed the mountain to Jerusalem, to the temple, on the pinnacle of Mount Zion. As they went, they sang these psalms of ascents. As they arrived and congregated from all directions, the singing would combine and become louder and louder. As they arrived at the gates of the temple, which was God's house, their songs were thanksgivings for what God had been doing for them. In fact, they brought thank-offerings with them for this purpose. They had entered His gates with thanksgiving, as Psalm 100 says. Then, as they went inside, the courtyard would become more and more crowded, and they would join in singing praises to God for His greatness. They had entered His courts with praise.

However, that was as far as they could go. They were not allowed inside, into the sanctuary, into the very presence of God. Only one man, the high priest, could go in there, once a year on the Day of Atonement, to atone for their sin. When he went in, it was silent. The sanctuary was off limits for the rest of the people. But it is not off limits for us today. In our true spiritual worship we are summoned to come right inside, not to an earthly replica of the holy place, but into heaven itself (Hebrews 9:24).

Certainly God is to be thanked, and God is to be praised. But thanks and praise are not unique to God; they can also be offered to people. However only God is to be worshipped. We today do not have to stop at the courts anymore; we are beckoned to come right into the presence of God, inside the holy place in heaven, because Christ our mediator and high priest is there on our behalf. We are now allowed to go all the way, so that we can give God the worship that He desires!

What does God want?

The apostle Paul told the heathen worshippers he met in Athens that God does not need anything from us. He is self-sufficient: *"The God who made the world and all things in it, since He is Lord of heaven and earth, does not dwell in temples made with hands; nor is He served by human hands, as though He needed anything, since He Himself gives to all people life and breath and all things"* (Acts 17:24,25).

However, God does desire something from us. He longs for the adoration of our hearts, the voluntary expression of our appreciation. Although it comes from our hearts, it flows out through our mouths. It is called *"a sacrifice of praise to God, that is, the fruit of lips that give thanks* [makes confession] *to His name"* (Hebrews 13:15).

God knows what is in our hearts of course, but He wants us to say it, to tell Him ourselves. And so we do it aloud, we speak our thanksgivings and meditations, and we sing praises together. We are "confessing" to God what we believe about Him and His Son.

So many times in the Bible, when people encountered the very presence of God, they fell on their faces. That is what John did, for example, when he saw the ascended and glorified person of Christ, even though He had been so familiar with Him when they were together on Earth. He fell down on his face *"like a dead man"* (Revelation 1:17). Worship involves complete awe and adoration of our majestic, almighty, eternal God. How much do we know about this kind of worship?

The Lord is not interested in our rituals or the procedures of our own invention that we may go through. He is interested in what is in our hearts. That does not mean that we can be careless in our actions or irreverent in our words, but neither is dry orthodoxy the answer, mere mindless compliance with ritual. For example, the epistle to the Hebrews says that we are to come *"with a sincere heart"* (Hebrews 10:22). Attitude, sincerity, and reverence are all-important.

Worship is not only an offering. It is in fact also a sacrifice, even though it does not involve us giving money or any material things. It certainly does not involve sacrificing the lives of animals, as used to be the case. But it does require serious thought and meditation, as well as preparation time beforehand in the Word of God. Psalm 45:1 describes the process: *"My heart overflows with a good theme; I address my verses to the King."* We do not just come to recite words from a prayer book or to produce lengthy dissertations. We come to express what God has given to us of an understanding and appreciation of Him and His Son. That takes forethought. The words that come out of our mouths should express what overflows from our hearts. This kind of worship will never be boring or routine.

Israel was instructed, *"Three times a year you shall celebrate a feast to Me. ...And none shall appear before Me empty-handed"* (Exodus 23:14,15). Similarly, we should never come into the presence of God without something that He values to offer to Him.

What pleases God?

How do we make sure that our worship pleases God? For example, is there anything that we know without a doubt really pleases Him? Yes there is, because He has said so, on more than one occasion. It is His own beloved Son. God His Father spoke out audibly from heaven about Christ on two separate occasions, once in the valley of the Jordan River and once on the mountain top, when He was being transfigured. Both times He said, *"This is my beloved Son, in whom I am well pleased"* (Matthew 3:17; 17:5).

God does not speak audibly from heaven very often and so this must be significant. It shows us that when we speak well of His Son, it is very pleasing to Him. And so now it is our turn to tell God that we too are well pleased in Him. When we present our appreciation of the excellencies of Christ to God His Father from genuine hearts, we know for certain that it will be acceptable. And here again, our worship about Christ is not primarily about what Christ has done for us; it is primarily about Him and what He means to God His Father.

What displeases God?

There are also things that we should avoid in our worship. For example, Israel was commanded not to add leaven or honey to their offerings (Leviticus 2:11). The lesson for us is that we must not mix in with our worship anything that is extraneous to what God commands, even though it might be appealing to us: *"Let us celebrate the feast, not with old leaven, nor with the leaven of malice and wickedness, but with the unleavened bread of sincerity and truth"* (1 Corinthians 5:8).

22.

The Worship of the Holy Priesthood

"So that with one accord you may with one voice glorify the God and Father of our Lord Jesus Christ."
(Romans 15:6)

Individually we should be living worshipful lives all the time, as the apostle Paul wrote to the church of God in Rome: *"Therefore I urge you, brethren, by the mercies of God, to present your bodies a living and holy sacrifice, acceptable to God, which is your spiritual service of worship"* (Romans 12:1). Much that we do for God personally is described as being an offering or a sacrifice that is pleasing to Him. But there is more to our worship than this.

Previously we saw that the house of God serves as a priesthood to God—not just individuals serving as priests, but a collective priesthood. We saw from the Old Testament that a primary job of the high priest was to represent the people as a whole. Christ is now high priest over the spiritual house of God (Hebrews 10:21), and He offers to His God and Father the worship of God's collective people (Hebrews 8:3). The unique privilege of being in the house of God is to be able to come into His presence as one people (even though gathered physically in different churches of God in different places). There is no closer relationship to God than worshipping in His presence. It is our crowning experience, and everything else flows from it.

Why say the "Amen"?

The words of praise and thanks that are spoken in worship are said by various individual men in the churches (1 Corinthians 14:34), as the saints gather for this purpose, but they are spoken on behalf of the whole congregation. The others express their participation in them by saying "Amen" (1 Corinthians 14:16), which means "let it be." Amen is the language of heaven, which is the place where God's will is always fully done (Revelation 19:4). It is also a title of the Lord Jesus, the one who always did His Father's will and gave Him all the glory (Revelation

3:14). A sincere and hearty "Amen" after an expression of thanksgiving and praise demonstrates that our worship is with one accord and one voice (Romans 15:6).

Therefore, an essential aspect of our worship is that it be done unitedly. The epistle to the Hebrews, in its climactic passage that describes our access to God in worship, stresses gathering together to do it: *"Let us draw near ... not forsaking our own assembling together"* (Hebrews 10:22,25).

As Christians we may possibly wish to confine ourselves to personal worship and not feel the need to join with others. We may think that this is sufficient and there is no need to be part of a group of people doing it together. Or we may think that it does not really matter with whom we worship. However, if that is the case, we will miss a lot of the privilege that God has provided for us. More importantly, it will leave out a lot of what He is looking for from us.

Is the Lord's Supper worship?

The Lord Jesus commanded His disciples to remember Him regularly by taking the emblems of bread and wine. In this way we proclaim His death until He comes back (1 Corinthians 11:26). When we do this, we honour Him and obey Him. It is by obeying His commands that we show our love for Him (John 13:35). The bread and the wine that we use are just symbols, nothing more, and yet they are full of meaning. They are designed to help us remember the reality of His body given and His blood poured out, and what they have accomplished. As we take them each time, we are intended to discern in our minds and hearts what they represent. Failing to do this is eating and drinking *"in an unworthy manner"* (1 Corinthians 11:27-30).

We have reviewed how Israel was never allowed beyond the veil (curtain) into the sanctuary, the most holy place, except for the high priest going in once a year on the Day of Atonement. But Christ has now gone into, and is still inside, the true holy place in heaven as our high priest. It says that He is our "forerunner" (Hebrews 6:20), and that He has gone in to appear there before the presence of God—*"for us"* (Hebrews 9:24). That is what makes it possible for us to come in as the holy priesthood—because He is there to mediate for us. He is a man in God's presence—and He is the only one there who has a body!

These verses state that we enter *"through the veil"*—not a physical curtain, but the humanity of Christ, who is alive there. With confidence based on His blood having been poured out at Calvary, and having been applied to us to deal forever with our sin, we draw near. It is these two things, His flesh and His blood, that are symbolized in the bread and wine.

"Since we have confidence to enter the holy place by the blood of Jesus, by a new and living way which He inaugurated for us through the veil, that is, His flesh, and since we have a great priest over the house of God, let us draw near ... " (Hebrews 10:19-22).

The way is now clear for us to come before God on His throne. What a privilege!

And so the Lord's Supper, the remembrance of the Lord Jesus, is not the epitome of worship by itself, but it initiates our priesthood worship in the presence of God, whereby we offer our spiritual sacrifices to God through Jesus Christ (1 Peter 2:5).

Is music worship?

In some Christian circles these days, it can seem that instrumental music is equated with worship. There are worship bands, worship leaders and worship performers. Does true worship require instrumental music?

Back in Old Testament days, instrumental music was an important part of Israel's service. For example, in preparation for the building of the temple, King David organized musicians for the service of the house, as described in 1 Chronicles 25. Yet the New Testament is silent on the subject of musical accompaniment for worship in God's house today. The whole emphasis is on singing from the heart (Ephesians 5:19). The sacrifice of praise is *"the fruit of lips"* (Hebrews 13:15).

The activity of offering spiritual sacrifices by a holy priesthood (1 Peter 2:5) is a matter of presenting to God expressions of thanksgiving and praise by speaking and singing to Him. This is not something that a worship leader can orchestrate; it must come spontaneously from our hearts. When we assemble for this purpose, it is for *"each one"* to offer, as 1 Corinthians 14:26 emphasizes. Hebrews 2:12 shows us that Christ Himself joins in our worship in heaven: *"In the midst of the congregation I will sing your praise."* There is a lot more to true worship than music. Instrumental music has nothing of value in itself to offer.

23.

To Whom Do We Speak in Worship?

"True worshipers will worship the Father ..." (John 4:23)

When we come to God to make requests, we pray to Him as our Father, because we're told that He is the one who answers our requests: *"Every good thing given and every perfect gift is from above, coming down from the Father"* (James 1:17).

But there is another expression for God the Father that has a unique and very special meaning. It is *"the God and Father of our Lord Jesus Christ."* It is a great thing that God is our God and is our Father, but it is much greater that He has those relationships with Christ. In worship it is His relationship with Christ that matters most.

As we saw previously, Christ's role in our worship is not to receive it for Himself, but to act as an intermediary between us and God His Father. The Holy Spirit's work is to enable us to offer it spiritually (Philippians 3:3). And so the entire godhead is involved when we worship (Ephesians 2:18).

A very special title

Christ often referred to God as His Father, but only three times does Scripture record that He called Him His "God." All three have to do with His humanity—because as a man, He had a God. The first of these was when He came to Earth at His incarnation: *"Then I said, 'Behold, I have come ... to do your will, O God'"* (Hebrews 10:7). The second was when He was on the cross, when He cried out, *"My God, my God, why have You forsaken me?"* (Matthew 27:46). And the third was at His resurrection, when He told Mary, *"I ascend to My Father and your Father, and My God and your God."* (John 20:17). These were three pivotal experiences for Him as a man in His earthly ministry, and each time He acknowledged that His Father was also His God. That involved His humanity.

It is particularly appropriate for us to address God with this title as the God and Father of our Lord Jesus Christ when we are worshipping Him. This elevates our approach to Him, by highlighting His relationship to Jesus Christ, rather than to us. Christ has saved us in order to produce worshippers for His God and Father (Revelation 1:6), because He knew that this is what His Father dearly wanted. Note that Revelation 1:6 refers to "His God," not just ours.

The expression of praise, "*Blessed be the God and Father of our Lord Jesus Christ ...,*" is used three times, twice by the apostle Paul and once by the apostle Peter (2 Corinthians 1:3; Ephesians 1:3; 1 Peter 1:3). It is an expression of exaltation and adoration. This is genuine worship.

What can we speak to God about?

In Revelation chapter 4 we are told that the apostle John was allowed to see into heaven, and there he saw wonderful things. He saw the majesty of God the Creator on His throne. What could be greater than that? That is the centre of everything. The wonders of God as Creator in all His wisdom and power are a very fitting subject matter for our worship: "*Worthy are You, our Lord and our God, to receive glory and honor and power; for You created all things, and because of Your will they existed, and were created*" (Revelation 4:11).

In the next chapter, John saw something even greater. He saw the Lamb of God, as though it had been newly killed, as the redeemer of mankind, and the only one qualified to carry out the righteous judgment of God. And so even the glory of God in creation is exceeded by the glory in His work of redemption. As far as we know, it did not cost God anything to create this world, but it cost Him His Son to redeem us. We can properly worship God for His great power and wisdom in what He has made, but we can especially worship Him for what He has done in saving us and bringing us to Himself through the work of Christ on Calvary: "*Worthy are You to take the book and to break its seals; for You were slain, and purchased for God with Your blood men from every tribe and tongue and people and nation. You have made them to be a kingdom and priests to our God; and they will reign upon the earth*" (Revelation 5:9,10).

John also saw myriads of angels engaged in worship. Hebrews 12:22 tells us that in the presence of God in worship there are innumerable hosts of angels. Revelation 4:8 tells us that they worship God day and night without rest. Isaiah also saw a vision of the throne of God, in His temple, where he saw the worship of angels:

> "*Seraphim stood above Him, each having six wings: with two he covered his face, and with two he covered his feet, and with two he flew. And one called out to another and said, Holy, Holy, Holy, is the LORD of hosts, the whole earth is full of His glory. And the foundations of the thresholds trembled at the voice of him who called out, while the temple was filling with smoke*" (Isaiah 6:2–4).

But no angel can worship as we can, for we are *"the redeemed of the Lord"* (Psalm 107:2). Angels cannot worship God for their salvation.

We will never exhaust appropriate material from the Scriptures for our offerings. The Lord Jesus said that all the Scriptures testify of Him (John 5:39). On the road to Emmaus He expounded in all the (Old Testament) Scriptures the things concerning Himself (Luke 24:27). David said in 1 Chronicles 29:14: *"of Your own we have given You."* The Scriptures are the source where we go for our meditations of Christ; they come from His own Word. But we can only give to God in expressions of worship what we already have received ourselves, and all of that comes initially from Him. That is what enables true worship.

24.

Lessons From King David

"David arose ... and he came into the house of the LORD and worshiped."
(2 Samuel 12:20)

David was Israel's greatest king. God called him a man after His own heart (1 Samuel 13:1) because he loved the same things that God loved. He loved God's house, as we saw earlier in Psalm 27. And in the well-known Psalm 23, he said: *"Surely goodness and loving-kindness will follow me all the days of my life, and I will dwell in the house of the LORD forever"* (verse 6).

David understood the heart of God, and He understood a lot about worship, even though he did not have the privilege that we can now have. And so let us look at some of the things that we can learn about worship from David's life.

It is not about appearances

"The LORD said to Samuel, 'Do not look at his appearance or at the height of his stature, because I have rejected him; for God sees not as man sees, for man looks at the outward appearance, but the LORD looks at the heart'" (1 Samuel 16:7).

When God was pointing out which son of Jesse He had chosen to be king in place of Saul, He passed over the obvious choices until he came to David, the youngest. Others were looking at external appearances—height, regal appearance, and "presence." But God was looking inside at the heart of each of the eight sons. And he chose David, because of what was in his heart.

When we worship, God does not look merely at our actions or listen to the eloquence of our words or the quality of our singing. He looks for what is coming from our hearts. We may enjoy some services more than others, perhaps when there are big crowds, high energy, or good singing performances, but God evaluates on a whole different basis. True worship is not about appearances.

It must be done God's way

"They placed the ark of God on a new cart that they might bring it from the house of Abinadab which was on the hill; and Uzzah and Ahio, the sons of Abinadab, were leading the new cart. So they brought it with the ark of God from the house of Abinadab, which was on the hill; and Ahio was walking ahead of the ark. Meanwhile, David and all the house of Israel were celebrating before the LORD with all kinds of instruments made of fir wood, and with lyres, harps, tambourines, castanets and cymbals. But when they came to the threshing floor of Nacon, Uzzah reached out toward the ark of God and took hold of it, for the oxen nearly upset it. And the anger of the LORD burned against Uzzah, and God struck him down there for his irreverence; and he died there by the ark of God. David became angry because of the LORD'S outburst against Uzzah, and that place is called Perez-uzzah to this day" (2 Samuel 6:3–8).

David keenly wanted to restore the Ark of the Covenant to its proper place in Jerusalem. It had been gone for a long time. He knew it represented the presence of God among His people. His predecessor, King Saul, had not paid attention to it, even though it had been stolen by the Philistines. As soon as he became king, David set about bringing the Ark back. But he was careless in how he did it. The Ark was heavy, and he used a cart drawn by oxen, the way the Philistines had carried it. David should have known better. God had prescribed that the Ark should only be transported on the shoulders of the Kohathites of the tribe of Levi (Numbers 4:15). It was to be covered and never touched directly. Yet Uzzah touched it while it was being transported, and he lost his life because of it. Uzzah was sincere in what he did, because he was afraid that the Ark might fall. But it was not allowed.

David learned the hard way that when we are dealing with things that are precious to God, they must be done God's way. The worship and service of God is holy, and is not to be treated lightly or carelessly. We are not at liberty to do it just as we think best, however sincere we may be.

The church of God in Corinth was warned that they were treating the Lord's supper in a casual way, and they were being disorderly. They were not observing God's divine order (1 Corinthians 11:17-22). God had judged them as a result, causing some of them to be sick and some even to die. They were warned therefore to examine themselves each time before they took of the bread and the cup, to be sure that they were properly discerning their meaning. True worship must be taken seriously.

It is not for spectators

"Then it happened as the ark of the LORD came into the city of David that Michal the daughter of Saul looked out of the window and saw King David leaping and dancing before the LORD; and she despised him in her heart" (2 Samuel 6:16).

David finally brought the Ark successfully to Jerusalem. He was so elated at this that he leaped and danced before it in public. He understood the significance of the occasion. But his wife, Michal, who was watching it all from a window, was disgusted at David's performance and thought that, as the king, he had degraded himself in the eyes of his subjects. From that time on, they were estranged from each other. They were not in agreement on this vital matter of the service of God.

David understood that worship is a participative activity. Watching or listening to other people praising God or speaking about God may be enjoyable, and even edifying, but it is not worship. One of the errors that came into the early churches in the first few centuries was the practice of leaving everything to a few people at the front (the clergy, the pastor, or the "professionals"), while the congregation basically acted as an audience. But we have been made to all function collectively as a priesthood, and to all be involved in offering the spiritual service. Worship is not for spectators.

In good times and bad

"When David saw that his servants were whispering together, David perceived that the child was dead; so David said to his servants, 'Is the child dead?' And they said, 'He is dead.' So David arose from the ground, washed, anointed himself, and changed his clothes; and he came into the house of the LORD and worshiped. Then he came to his own house, and when he requested, they set food before him and he ate" (2 Samuel 12:19,20).

Sometimes we may not feel like worshipping God or coming together to keep His remembrance in the Lord's Supper. We may be discouraged or may be going through difficult times. We may be preoccupied with our own problems and may not feel like doing it. But if we allow our variable emotional state to dictate our actions, we will be very irregular in our service. David had just experienced a huge trauma, the loss of his newborn son, due to his sin with Bathsheba. He had pleaded with God to spare the boy's life, but to no avail. When David was finally told that his son was dead, he must have been devastated. Yet His first action was to prepare himself and go to the house of the Lord and worship, even though it was God who had taken his son.

If it had happened to us, we might have been angry at the Lord because He could have spared the boy's life. But not so with David. He immediately went and worshipped, despite how he may have felt. David understood worship.

There is a cost

> *"The king said to Araunah, 'No, but I will surely buy it from you for a price, for I will not offer burnt offerings to the LORD my God which cost me nothing.' So David bought the threshing floor and the oxen for fifty shekels of silver. David built there an altar to the LORD and offered burnt offerings and peace offerings"* (2 Samuel 24:24,25).

David went up to offer to the Lord in order to stop a plague that had been caused by his sin in numbering the people. He went up Mount Moriah, the same place where Abraham had gone to offer Isaac about a thousand years before. David knew that he was going to the right place, but the site belonged to a Jebusite named Araunah. Araunah was willing to donate it to the king, but David would not allow it. He knew that an offering to God that had not cost him anything was not of any value. He insisted on paying for it.

So it is with us. Our worship to God is referred to as a sacrifice—*"spiritual sacrifices"* (1 Peter 2:5). There are personal costs involved. It takes time to study and meditate. There may be time or cost for travelling to the assembly gathering. It may in some cases involve ridicule, or overcoming apathy or resistance from others. It certainly involves self-denial in living holy lives, and in confessing sins that we commit. If what we bring to God in worship has not cost us anything, how much is it worth? We must be sure that we are not just giving God our left-overs.

25.

How Can We "Come Clean"?

"Who may ascend into the hill of the LORD?
Or who may stand in His holy place?
He who has clean hands and a pure heart."
(Psalm 24:3,4)

When King Hezekiah came to the throne of Judah at age twenty-five, things were in disarray (2 Chronicles 29). The temple was in disuse and disrepair. Idolatry was rampant throughout the country. The nation was losing its distinct identity as the people on whom God had placed His name; they were being assimilated into the surrounding culture. The feast days and holy convocations were not taking place. The annual Passover was not being kept. The priests and the Levites were not engaged in the temple service. Nor were they being supported financially by the people as they should have been; instead they were engaged in purely secular activity. The nation was under the constant threat of the cruel Assyrians from the northeast. There had been numerous casualties among the people, and many had been taken captive. Hezekiah's father had tried to compromise with the Assyrians to pacify them, but had failed miserably. The people were disorganized and disheartened.

This was rather a big challenge for a twenty-five year-old. As he took the throne, Hezekiah realized that a massive clean-up was necessary. He organized an intensive sixteen-day work program. The temple and its courts were cleaned thoroughly and repaired. The priests and Levites were restored to active service. But even when he was finished, Hezekiah knew that worship could not take place until cleansing for the people's past sin had taken place. It could not be ignored. And so, on the seventeenth day, he got up early in the morning and made arrangements for something that he knew had to happen first. He gave the command for sin offerings to be offered. The people had sinned, and He knew that, in God's things, we cannot just ignore sins and move on. Hezekiah commanded the people to sacrifice bulls and lambs and goats as a sin-offering to atone for their sins. He knew how important cleansing was before coming into the presence of God. The people had to "come clean."

Today we never need to offer sin offerings. The last (and only effective) sin offering was Christ's death on the cross. His blood cleanses us from all sin: *"The blood of Jesus His Son cleanses us from all sin"* (1 John 1:7). His work on Calvary is sufficient.

Cleansing of our consciences

None of the Old Testament animal sacrifices that was offered over the centuries could ever permanently remove the people's sin. The people knew that their sins had been dealt with in the prescribed way, but they did not realize that this was only a temporary covering until the one effective sin offering would be made to take them away forever (Hebrews 10:12). *"Both gifts and sacrifices are offered which cannot make the worshiper perfect in conscience, since they relate only to food and drink and various washings, regulations for the body imposed until a time of reformation ... "* (Hebrews 9:9,10).

But now the single offering of Christ has been made which has totally cleansed our consciences to enable us to come near in worship: *"... For if the blood of goats and bulls and the ashes of a heifer sprinkling those who have been defiled sanctify for the cleansing of the flesh, how much more will the blood of Christ, who through the eternal Spirit offered Himself without blemish to God, cleanse your conscience from dead works to serve the living God?"* (Hebrews 9:13,14)

As a result, when we approach God in our worship in the holy place in heaven, we are able to do so because the blood of Christ has been applied to cleanse our hearts forever. Our consciences are now clean: *"Let us draw near with a sincere heart in full assurance of faith, having our hearts sprinkled clean from an evil conscience ... "* (Hebrews 10:22). We no longer have to deal with the problem of guilt for our sin.

Cleansing for fellowship

1 John 1:9 tells us to confess the sins that we continue to commit: *"If we confess our sins, He is faithful and righteous to forgive us our sins and to cleanse us from all unrighteousness"*. This was written to believers, as 1 John 5:13 shows: *"These things I have written to you who believe in the name of the Son of God."*

Since we are already eternally saved from the guilt of our sins, why is this confession of on-going sin necessary? It is because sin of any kind keeps us apart from God. It breaks our fellowship with Him. The only thing that will bring us back into close fellowship again is repentance and confession, and we must never overlook the need for that. We need constantly to be on the alert for sin occurring in our lives, so that we might confess it and be cleansed from it. This is a prerequisite for our worship and service. *"The eyes of the Lord are toward the righteous, and His ears attend to their prayer, but the face of the Lord is against those who do evil"* (1 Peter 3:12).

Cleansing from defilement

Even after our sins have been dealt with, there is another problem, the fact that we become defiled in our everyday lives, simply through contact with the world, which is a defiled place. Nothing that is defiled can enter the presence of God (Habakkuk 1:13). Our minds are particularly vulnerable to thoughts that are contaminated by exposure to the world around us. This need for cleansing from defilement is something that we also need to remind ourselves about constantly, about how seriously God regards any taint in the lives of His people. We may tend to become rather tolerant and blasé about it, and certainly the world's standards will not help us here.

We can also become very good at trying to justify our own actions, but the Lord has said: *"To this one I will look, to him who is humble and contrite of spirit, and who trembles at My word"* (Isaiah 66:2). The apostle Paul exhorted the Corinthians: *"Let us cleanse ourselves from all defilement of flesh and spirit, perfecting holiness in the fear of God"* (2 Corinthians 7:1).

Constant cleansing from defilement is a prerequisite if we are to enjoy the presence of the Lord. It is very significant that the Lord Jesus washed His apostles' feet in the upper room before He introduced His remembrance to them (John 13:5). As He was doing so He said to Peter, *"If I do not wash you, you have no part with Me"* (John 13:8). He did not wash their feet because of any sin that they had committed, but because their feet were dirty from walking in the world outside. In a similar way, the Old Testament priests' feet always had to be washed at the laver before they went inside the tabernacle or temple (Exodus 30:17).

While sin can only be cleansed by the application of the blood of Christ (through confession), defilement from the world is cleansed through the application of "the water of the Word" of God (Ephesians 5:26). Psalm 119:9,11 says, *"How can a young man keep his way pure? By keeping it according to Your word ... Your word I have treasured in my heart, that I may not sin against You"*. It is by spending time in God's Word that we cleanse our minds of the natural defiling effects of living in a godless world. It changes our focus and corrects our thinking, as well as making us conscious of any sin that needs to be confessed. This cleansing prepares us for the act of worship.

Defilement due to unresolved conflicts

Because worship in God's house is collective, our relationships with one other are vitally important. Any inter-personal conflicts between us must be put right first. Inter-personal difficulties inhibit true worship: *"If someone says, 'I love God,' and hates his brother, he is a liar; for he who does not love his brother whom he has seen, how can he love God whom he has not seen?"* (1 John 4:20). For example, when the apostles were on their way to the upper room, they had been debating who among them would be the greatest (Luke 22:24), which is hardly the state of mind to be in to keep the Lord's Supper.

The Lord Jesus spoke about what a worshipper should do when he or she is aware that another person is in conflict with them: *"If you are presenting your offering at the altar, and there remember that your brother has something against you, leave your offering there before the altar and go; first be reconciled to your brother, and then come and present your offering"* (Matthew 5:23,24). Personal reconciliation is an urgent priority, and failure to attend to it impairs the service of God. Even though the worshipper in this case was not the one with the problem, he was still expected to take the initiative to get it sorted out. Similarly, the apostle Paul stressed to the saints in Rome the need to persevere in being on good terms with each other for their worship to be effective (Romans 15:5,6).

Defilement due to divided loyalties

Israel's worst sin was not murder or adultery, as serious as they were. It was idolatry. It broke the first commandment: *"You shall have no other gods before me"* (Exodus 20:3). It involved them giving God's unique place as the one who should receive all worship to someone or something else, to a created thing. The worst instance of idolatry was when the devil, who was a created angel, expected Christ, God the Son, to fall down and worship him when he tempted Him in the wilderness: *"He said to Him, 'All these things I will give You, if You fall down and worship me.' Then Jesus said to him, 'Go, Satan! For it is written, you shall worship the Lord your God, and serve Him only'"* (Matthew 4:9,10).

Anytime we substitute anything in the place of God we are committing idolatry, and it is something we must carefully guard against. In the book of Revelation, when the apostle John had seen all the marvellous visions of the future, he was so impressed that he began to worship the angel that had showed them to him. But the angel stopped him abruptly with the words *"Worship God"* (Revelation 19:10). God alone is to be worshipped. One of the evidences of the deity of Christ is that during His lifetime He never prevented anyone from worshipping

Him (Matthew 14:33; 28:9; John 9:38). If He had not been God, that would have been idolatrous.

Defilement due to conflicting priorities

But the problem in Israel was not only worshipping false gods. It was that at times they claimed to be continuing to worship God as well. They wanted it both ways, and that is impossible. That is why Elijah said to them: *"If the LORD is God, follow Him; but if Baal, follow him"* (1 Kings 18:21). This practice of trying to mix two incompatible beliefs is called "syncretism." In our commitment to the Lord, it is not enough for us to be doing the right things, such as participating in church services, reading our Bibles, and praying. We must also stop doing the wrong things, things that contradict or interfere. James in his epistle said that a double-minded person is unstable and will not receive anything from the Lord (James 1:7,8). True worship is single minded.

Defilement due to misplaced focus

We may tend to be attracted to things that we can look at and visualize, even in our service for God. But we need to take care that they do not themselves become the focus of our worship. The second of the ten commandments given to Israel at Sinai prohibited any images from being made and worshipped: *"You shall not make for yourself an idol, or any likeness of what is in heaven above or on the earth beneath or in the water under the earth"* (Exodus 20:4).

God knew very well our human tendency to want visual things to stimulate our minds and how potentially dangerous this can be. So He forbade them. The brass serpent, which had been raised by Moses in the wilderness when the people of Israel were dying from a plague, was kept by them. They should have destroyed it, because centuries later it became an object of worship (2 Kings 18:4). It is a natural tendency.

Today some churches use relics and images to stimulate reverence. But, as Paul told the people of Athens, God is not worshipped by things men make with their hands (Acts 17:25). He wants to be worshipped in spirit and truth. He Himself is to be our focus. True worship is invisible, but it is very real.

Defilement due to reliance on ritual

Towards the end of the Old Testament, God sent word to His people that He was displeased with their offerings because they were not bringing their best. Their heart was not in their worship, and He hated it. He said to them: *"Oh that there were one among you who would shut the gates, that you might not uselessly kindle fire on My altar! I am not pleased with you,' says the LORD of hosts, 'nor will I accept an offering from you'"* (Malachi 1:10). Even though the people were still engaging in all the activity, God wanted it to stop. They were just going through the motions. It was not acceptable to Him.

In a similar way, the Lord told the Pharisees that their offerings were not acceptable because they were offering to God money that the law required should have been used to care for parents (Matthew 15:5,6). When we disobey God, we cannot compensate by offering God service. It does not work that way.

And so, if we are to "come clean" in our approach to God in worship, we must examine our hearts and our lives and put right those things that will disqualify our worship. True worship is offered by clean worshippers.

"Search me, O God, and know my heart; try me and know my anxious thoughts; and see if there be any hurtful way in me" (Psalm 139:23,24)

26.

True Worship—A Summary

Let us now summarize the main points of this section on the subject of true worship:

- God alone deserves our worship and He desires it from us.

- Not all worship is acceptable to Him. He has told us in His Word what He desires.

- Worship is more than thanking God for what He has done for us; it especially involves praising Him and expressing our awe and adoration of Him for what He is and does.

- Nothing pleases God more than us expressing to Him genuine appreciation of His Son.

- True worship is offered, not by physical means in physical places, but in spirit and truth.

- Gospel preaching, sermons, instrumental music, and good works are for people's benefit, but true worship is directed to God and gives Him what He wants.

- God wants audible worship, speaking and singing aloud what comes from our hearts.

- God does not want rituals. He is looking for genuine, devout, informed confession of His name to Him.

- Our highest privilege as disciples today is to engage in the collective offering of spiritual sacrifices to the God and Father of the Lord Jesus.

- This collective worship is offered by the holy priesthood of the house of God. The offerings are made acceptable to God through the high priestly service of Jesus Christ in heaven.

- The remembrance of the Lord Jesus in the bread and wine initiates this collective worship.

- Many things can interfere with true worship, such as failure to confess sin, defilement from worldly influences, and unresolved inter-personal conflict. We need to make it a priority to correct these things in order that our worship not be invalidated.

Conclusion

What are We Missing?

We have now come to the end of our study. It is therefore time to try to draw together the various strands of what we have been looking at to draw some overall conclusions.

We began by exploring the glorious subject of God wanting to have a house on Earth among men and women, and that today it is intended to consist of people themselves and not physical structures. It is a spiritual house and it enjoys marvellous privileges, but there are also some important conditions attached. We saw that we should not assume, because we are believers in Christ and therefore eternally members of the church that is Christ's Body, that we are automatically in the house of God or that we can share in these privileges. There is more to it than that.

Then we saw that the practical requirement was for an identifiable people to be gathered together on Earth, and we examined God's prescription for this. We explored God's churches, beginning with the first ones in New Testament times, looking for the underlying pattern that He laid down for us to apply today. We saw that they were of God's own design and saints were in them because of His calling, not theirs. We saw again that there are great privileges and important requirements, and that the Lord is quite specific in His Word about how He wants these things done. We should not just assume therefore that any gathering of believers is automatically a church of God, or is part of His spiritual house.

Then we explored the supreme act of service to God, which is true worship. And we asked the questions: "What worship does God consider acceptable?" and "What can we offer that pleases Him?" We saw that more was involved than individual acts of worship, and we delved into the wonder of being allowed to worship together in spirit and truth in heaven itself as the holy priesthood.

Unity and the truth

In all this, we saw an emphasis on togetherness and collectivity. This does not downplay in any way the importance of our individual devotion and service to the Lord, but it shows the framework within which they should be applied. God is a God of unity. The godhead itself is united, three distinct persons in complete

141

harmony. God always joins things that are alike, and separates things that are different, just as He did at creation. He is not a God of mixtures or of compromise. Independence and isolation are not divine characteristics. He desires all of us as believers, with all our inherent diversity, to be harmonized through the work of His Spirit to become a complete reflection of His own Son, because He is the One in whom His Father gets His full delight.

But God is also a God of truth. He will not compromise His truth for the sake of unity. It must be *"the unity of the faith."* Otherwise it would be a false unity, a facade. Believers who differ on fundamental teachings of Scripture, or who operate in isolation from each other, cannot function as one. They cannot worship collectively. This unity is much more than an aggregation of individuals, such as separate body parts. It is like a complete body which is operating with all its faculties fully coordinated.

This all has to do with our identity, who we are for God. It is all about our particular relationships with Him, and the spiritual position that we have been given. The privileges and the obligations flow from the position. [27] Neglecting either our spiritual condition or our position results in a relationship that is sadly lacking. We must be concerned with both.

We have seen and enjoyed the fact that each believer is eternally a member of the church the Body of Christ, an indissoluble union that can never be taken away or spoiled. In that spiritual reality, we are one, but we have also seen that becoming a member of it is not the end of our spiritual journey but rather a necessary starting point. The essential point for us is that this oneness needs to be reflected in practice in the way that God has prescribed.

We have discovered that God intends disciples of the Lord Jesus in these days to be gathered together in a community, linked place by place, in full adherence to all of the Lord's teaching for us, as revealed through His Word by the Holy Spirit. He calls those gatherings "churches of God." It was to disciples gathered in this way that the New Testament epistles were written and to whom they applied. It would be presumptuous of us to say that what was written to them also applies to us today if we are not similarly gathered together by God.

---

27 Marriage illustrates this point. God has provided the relationship of marriage for men and women, in which He intends love and intimacy to be expressed. When a husband and wife enter into the position of being a married couple, God joins them, but the ongoing quality of that marriage depends on the love they show within it. Neither intimacy without the commitment of marriage, nor a loveless marriage, fulfills what God designed.

How the Body grows up

The practical implication of us being members of the Body of Christ on Earth is that we are inter-dependent—dependent on Christ our Head, and on one another. We are each intended to serve a particular purpose, and we have been equipped by Him to do it. We need each other, and we need to be properly connected to each other, in order to fulfill this purpose. If any Body part is missing, disjointed, or not fulfilling its assigned part, the whole is weakened.

How then are we to mature towards this "measure of the stature of the fullness of Christ?" The prescription for this is given, as we have seen, in chapter 4 of Ephesians, verses 11 to 16:

- Each of us is to carefully avoid all wrong teaching, and instead speak the truth of God to each other in love.

- We are to apply this truth to ourselves, and so grow up in Christ.

- As each one of us receives the enabling grace from Christ, we should minister to those we have contact with, also in love.

- We should all aspire to continue this process until we reach a mutual and correct understanding and application of the teaching of the Lord in our lives, and a full enjoyment of every aspect of our relationship with Him.

For us as living members of the Body of Christ to truly aspire to this goal, it is necessary to learn and put into practice the truths from Scripture that we have been discovering.

Knowledge and information about the things of God requires diligent study of the Scriptures these days, usually aided by competent teachers, which God supplies. But what is also needed is a deep heart conviction about these things, which gives rise to a passion to apply them fully in our lives. Even after we have acquired the knowledge, and all our questions have been answered, that conviction and passion can only come from God Himself. If we are sincerely seeking after God's truth, we will earnestly ask for it (Hebrews 11:6).

The obligation of revelation

When God shows us a truth from Scripture, it puts us under two obligations. Firstly, it obligates us to live it, to put it into practice ourselves. Otherwise it will be nothing more than a theory. God does not entrust us with a revelation of His truth just so that we might know about it, or to satisfy our curiosity. Secondly, it obligates us to share it with others as we have opportunity, since that is the means that God normally uses to spread His truth.

If what has been covered in the pages of this book is indeed according to the mind of God, then it leaves each one of us with certain inescapable conclusions:

- If the church I am associated with does not adhere faithfully to the full teaching of the Lord, in active fellowship with all other such churches, it cannot be a scriptural "church of God."

- If I am not in a church of God, I cannot be part of God's house on Earth, nor in the kingdom of God.

- If I am not in the house of God, I cannot participate in the collective heavenly sanctuary worship of the holy priesthood, which is the pinnacle of human experience and service today.

- If I am not in God's church, not in God's house, and not able to engage in this true worship, I am obviously missing something very vital in my Christian experience, no matter what else of value I may be doing.

If this is in fact the case, the answer to the overriding question of this book, "Am I Missing Something?" would have to be a resounding "yes!" This may sound distressing, and yet it can be the starting point for wonderful advancement in the things of God.

If God does in fact have a particular way that He wants disciples to gather, why would I want to be anywhere else, regardless of whatever natural attraction other places may have? We all have our own personal preferences about things and our comfort zones. And we can so easily make implicit assumptions about things in Scripture, without checking them out to be sure. One purpose of this book has been to challenge some of those assumptions, as they have been challenged in my own life, to force us to examine what the Scriptures really say and really mean. The test of our faith, then, will be our willingness to act on what is revealed to us.

Our natural tendency may be to accept things that are familiar to us, until they are challenged, or until an issue affects us personally. Even then, we can tend to change our beliefs and convictions only grudgingly. We don't normally do it just because someone else tells us to, or because a different point of view is presented. We do it because we have discovered it for ourselves, at a time in our life when it is important to us, when the answers matter to us. Discovering these answers for ourselves can be hard work. There is no shortcut.

Does it matter?

It is important to keep in mind that these are not just fine points of difference between Christians, debatable points of theology, things that are of secondary importance. These are fundamental issues about who we are and what we do as followers of Jesus Christ. They are of supreme importance to the Lord Himself. We know how He feels about these things. For example, we know about His zeal for God's house, by how He reacted to the money-changers in the temple when they were abusing it. We know how He feels about the church of God, because of how He took Saul's persecution of it so personally. And we know how He feels about true worship, because He died in order to make it possible for us to be a priesthood to His God and Father. The whole subject is at the very heart of the things of God. Paul told the elders of Ephesus that the church of God is something "… *which He purchased with His own blood*"—literally, "the blood of His own" (Acts 20:28).

This book is sent out as an appeal to my fellow members of the Body of Christ out of a deep conviction that many believers today may be unaware of these vital truths, even though they may be greatly pleasing to the Lord in their devotion to the truths that have been shown to them. It is when we are obedient to what we already know that God tends to show us more. There are disciples today who are putting into practice these glorious truths, and who long to share them with others.

If this book causes any believer to examine these things from God's Word, openly and humbly, it will have served its purpose. To that end, I pray:

"… that in all things God may be glorified through Jesus Christ, to whom belong the glory and the dominion forever and ever" (1 Peter 4:11).

The author invites comments and enquiries:

E-mail: kdpublications@zing-net.ca
or
Mail: KD Publications, 34 Eversley Hall, King City, ON, Canada L7B 1L8

Website: www.kdpublications.com

Appendices

A.

The Standard of Truth

"Be diligent to present yourself approved to God as a workman who does not need to be ashamed, accurately handling the word of truth." (2 Timothy 2:15)

As we seek to discover more of God's truth, we need a fundamental standard or criterion to apply. Just as the Reformers applied the expression "sola scriptura", so for us the inspired Scriptures must be the ultimate criterion. But we must properly understand them, which requires that we apply proper principles to guide us as we come to them for answers. Here are some examples of such principles.

The authority of Scripture

First, we must accept the total authority of Scripture. We must accept that the Bible with its sixty-six books is the uniquely inspired Word of God (2 Timothy 3:16). It is "verbally inspired," meaning that the original words themselves came from God, although they were written down by men. That means that we can be very particular in our examination of the actual words used (in the original texts), and their meaning, within their various contexts.

This inspiration means that the Bible can be entirely trusted to be accurate and reliable, without error in the original. Research into early manuscripts has been thorough enough to give us very strong assurance that the Bible we read today in English and other major languages is substantially without error.

The Bible alone is the Word of God. It is unique. Psalm 138:2 states: *"You have magnified Your word according to all Your name,"* which shows the place that God's Word has with God Himself. The Lord Jesus said: *"Heaven and earth will pass away, but My words will not pass away"* (Matthew 24:35).

While there are many other religious books in the world, and also many very helpful books about the Bible, such as Bible study aids, these do not have the same status as the Scriptures. Every other writing, saying or proposition must be tested against the Bible itself. Where it is found to be at variance it must be rejected. This also means that, even although it was written long ago, the Bible is relevant and sufficient in itself. Any fundamental teaching that goes beyond what the Bible itself presents must also be rejected (1 Corinthians 4:6).

Much of what is believed and practised in the Christian world these days is based on tradition. In fact it is an article of faith in the Orthodox churches and the Roman Catholic church that the church traditions may have, in practice, equal weight with the Scriptures. However, not all tradition is bad. In fact, the apostle Paul wrote to the church in Thessalonica: *"So then, brethren, stand firm and hold to the traditions which you were taught, whether by word of mouth or by letter from us"* (2 Thessalonians 2:15). However we must very carefully consider what our traditions are based on. Again, we must apply the test of Scripture. The Lord Jesus criticized the Jewish leaders in His day when He said to them: *"You have made the commandment of God of no effect by your tradition"* (Matthew 15:6 NKJV). He said that they were *"teaching as doctrines the precepts of men"* (Matthew 15:9).

While it can be very difficult for us to change what we have long held to be true, we must come to the Scriptures with an open heart and mind if we are to expect the Spirit of God to show us His truth. Traditions to be rejected are those which have been devised by men, no matter how well intentioned. Traditions inspired by God, as Paul's were, are to be held.

The interpretation of Scripture

Scripture can only be understood through the inner working of the Holy Spirit. It is *"the sword of the Spirit"* (Ephesians 6:17). Spiritual things can only be discerned spiritually, not just by natural intellect (1 Corinthians 2:14). A willingness to understand them and then humbly do them is the prerequisite. It is not just a matter of academic study.

Even though scriptural truth is absolute, we must be carful that we are properly interpreting it within its context, *"accurately handling the word of truth"* (2 Timothy 2:15). Accurate handling is important because it is possible to misuse the Scriptures (2 Peter 3:16), either deliberately or accidentally. What it means to one person is also what it must mean to others; it cannot be interpreted differently for different people: *"No prophecy of Scripture is a matter of one's own interpretation"* (2 Peter 1:20). Thus, just as the parts of the human body are all inter-dependent and cannot work properly without each other, so the various portions of Scripture are inter-dependent. They cannot be explained in isolation or out of context; one explains the other.

The Old Testament and New Testament

In the New Testament we are told that the Old Testament Scriptures were written with us today in mind, and that *"they were written for our admonition"* (1 Corinthians 10:11). It says: *"whatever was written in earlier times was written for our instruction, so that by perseverance and the encouragement of the Scriptures we might have hope"* (Romans 15:4).

The Old Testament sets out principles and illustrations for us today. God Himself never changes, but how He deals with people has changed from the old covenant to the new covenant. We today therefore take our direction from the New Testament Scriptures. But relevant Old Testament passages illuminate them and tutor us to see Christ and His teaching for us today (Galatians 3:24). When this takes place we find that divine principles are unchanging (see for example 1 Corinthians 14:34).

These principles and illustrations from the Old Testament are particularly helpful on matters that also have application today under the new covenant. The book of Hebrews, for example, makes extensive reference by comparison and contrast to the old covenant priesthood and tabernacle service to teach about service in the house of God today.

English language translations

English-speaking readers of the Bible are blessed with a ready supply of translations, thanks to an abundance of scholarship and effort that has gone into producing highly reliable versions of Scripture in their language. New translations continue to be produced. However it is important to realize that even the best of translations include an element of interpretation by the translators. This is because idioms and figures of speech are used, both in the original languages and in the languages into which they are being translated, and so a word-for-word conversion would not be meaningful. In addition, the meaning of words in our English language is constantly changing.

For example, the King James Version of 1611 refers to God having *"a peculiar people"* (1 Peter 2:9), meaning that the people belong exclusively to Him. Today however the word "peculiar" tends to be used primarily in a way which means "odd" or "eccentric". The words *"a peculiar people"* have been changed in the more recent (1983) New King James Version (NKJV) to *"His own special people"* in an attempt to keep up to date with this trend. Extensive research into the original documents over the past two hundred years has resulted in relatively few changes to our Bible. Most of the changes in newer versions are the result of updating to new idiom and expressions.

It is virtually impossible to undertake a translation without introducing implicit assumptions about the meaning of the text, despite extremely thorough attempts by translation teams to eliminate bias. The aim of some translations is ease of readability for the average reader; others aim for precision for the Bible student. One of the most precise versions still available, although it is less readable these days, is the Revised Version, both the English (1885) and American (1901) editions.

In this book, wherever the common English translation of a Bible text could potentially be misleading with respect to a point being made, an explanation has been given for the words which are used in the original language.

The importance of "the"

One recurring example of translation variation is where the definite article ("the") appears in the Greek text of the New Testament, but is not translated as such in the English, and vice versa. It is a small word, but one which can make an important difference. Generally, the definite article does not appear as frequently in Greek as it does in English, and instead it is often implied. However, where it does occur, it makes the word to which it applies more definite (hence the name "definite article"). We therefore need to consider its use, as it can significantly affect the meaning of a sentence.

An example of this is in Acts 2:42, which the NKJV expresses as: "*And they continued steadfastly in the apostles' doctrine and fellowship, in the breaking of bread, and in prayers.*" Four things are mentioned here, and the definite article is attached to two of them. However, in the original Greek text, the definite article appears with all four of them. It is "*the fellowship*" (meaning a single defined community of disciples), not just "fellowship with." And it is "*the prayers*" (meaning a defined gathering for prayer), not just the general activity of praying. These distinctions are important if we are to "*accurately handle the word of truth.*"

The same is true with respect to the omission of the definite article. For example, the NKJV translates 1 Corinthians 3:16 and 12:27 as "*you are the temple of God*" and "*you are the body of Christ.*" But the definite article is not in either of those texts in the original Greek, because "the church of God" at Corinth to whom Paul addressed these statements (1 Corinthians 1:1) was not synonymous with either "the temple of God" or "the Body of Christ." They were just a portion of them, and the apostle was emphasizing what they were a part of in order to show them that they should act in a way that was characteristic of them. And so, more correctly, these verses could be translated "*you are* [of the] *temple of God*" and "*you are* [of the] *body of Christ.*" Otherwise we may draw the wrong conclusion that the terms "church of God," "temple of God," and "Body of Christ" are synonymous. Therefore the little word "the" can make a big difference to the meaning of a Scripture by its presence or absence.

Distinctions in meaning

Other distinctions include how particular words are translated. One example is in 1 Corinthians 3:9, where the expression occurs in the NKJV, the New International Version (NIV), and the New American Standard Bible (NASB) *"you are God's field."* Yet the original Greek text for the word "field" uses the word *"georgion,"* which means a "husbandry," a marked-out piece of ground that is tilled and cared for by a gardener (such as the garden of Eden). This is quite different from a wide-open field, where plants grow wild, especially since the symbolism of a field in Scripture is of the world outside (Matthew 13:38). In this Scripture the apostle Paul was not telling the saints in the church of God at Corinth that they were part of the world, but that they were a defined garden belonging to God. Since the very words of Scripture are God given, we need to be careful as to what they actually mean.

"Sola scriptura"

This motto of the Reformers in the fourteenth to sixteenth Centuries, "by the Scriptures alone," was a paramount principle for them. It helped them to break out of the limitations of the church's traditional interpretation of the Scriptures. The statement *"The unfolding of Your words gives light; it gives understanding to the simple"* (Psalm 119:130) was true then and is still true today. It was when people began to have access to the Scriptures themselves, and not just to the church's interpretation of them, and when God's Word began to penetrate their minds and hearts, that the truth of God began to be rediscovered.

Doctrine starts with the letters "do"—we are not just to know it but to do it. Being given an understanding of the Word of God puts the onus on us to be obedient to it. The Word of truth, properly understood, must be the ultimate test of what we believe and what we actually do. That is what we will answer for. Revelation brings its obligations—to live it, and then to share it.

B.

What is "The Faith"?

"Test yourselves to see if you are in the faith; examine yourselves!"
(2 Corinthians 13:5)

When writing to the church in Ephesus the apostle Paul warned them about being *"carried about by every wind of doctrine"* (Ephesians 4:14). Later he wrote to Timothy, using a similar metaphor, about some people who had *"suffered shipwreck in regard to their faith"* (1 Timothy 1:19). The danger he was describing is that believers may be taken off course in their Christian lives and service by wrong teaching. It is just as much a risk for us today, since there are so many different teachings in the religious world, even among Christian denominations. It is quite possible for us to be deceived or led astray.

"The faith" is an expression used in Scripture to refer to the whole body of teaching given by the Lord to His apostles, and then taught by them to be carried out. It is the same thing as *"the apostles' teaching"* that the early disciples continually devoted themselves to (Acts 2:42). *"Faith"* is believing something; *"the faith"* is the truth that is to be believed. By the end of the New Testament period, the faith had been delivered to the saints by the apostles in its entirety, and it was not to be added to:

> *"Beloved, while I was making every effort to write you about our common salvation, I felt the necessity to write to you appealing that you contend earnestly for the faith which was once for all handed down to the saints"* (Jude verse 3).

We do not need a new doctrinal foundation today. The original faith taught by the apostles is still entirely relevant and sufficient for us.

The faith is described as a "mystery"—truth that can be revealed only by God (1 Timothy 3:9), which helps to explain why it is not universally understood or accepted.

The apostle Paul told Titus to make sure that the saints were *"sound in the faith"* (Titus 1:13). He said that some people had *"wandered away"* from it, and that some would *"fall away"* from it (1 Timothy 6:10; 4:1). At the end of his life, he said that he himself had *"kept the faith"* (2 Timothy 4:7). One of the possible dangers of having only a single minister or authority in a particular church is that his own views can become predominant. The counsel of others is often needed to discern the mind of the Lord: *"Iron sharpens iron, so one man sharpens another"* (Proverbs 27:17).

A primary goal for us as living members of the church the Body of Christ is to attain to *"the unity of the faith"* (Ephesians 4:13)—where we as believers in Christ are all faithfully carrying out His entire teaching in fellowship with one other. This unity does not refer to some form of compromise or ecumenical association that ignores or downplays differences of views and beliefs. It is active and willing obedience, based on a full understanding of what the Lord is looking for from us today. That, and nothing less, should be the aspiration of all of us as believers. It is the basis on which we can put into practice the realities of God's house and God's church that we have been looking at. Since it is in fact "the faith," it is vital that we believe it and be fully convinced about it.

Following is a brief summary of some prevalent wrong teachings, contrasted with "the faith" of Scripture:

"EVERY WIND OF DOCTRINE"	"THE FAITH"
THE BIBLE	
The Bible contains errors. Parts of it are not authentic. Other "holy books" have equal or greater status.	All the words in the original text of the books of the Bible came from God and are totally accurate and reliable. The Bible is unique; all other writings must be tested against it. • *"Your word is truth"* (John 17:17). • *"All Scripture is inspired by God and profitable for teaching, for reproof, for correction, for training in righteousness"* (2 Timothy 3:16). • *"Until heaven and earth pass away, not the smallest letter or stroke shall pass from the Law until all is accomplished"* (Matthew 5:18).

THE PERSON OF GOD	
There is no god. There are many gods. Everything is god. Jesus Christ was not eternally God the Son. The Holy Spirit is just an influence, not a person of the godhead.	There is one true and living God, in three persons—Father, Son (Jesus Christ), and Holy Spirit. • *"There is one God."* (1 Timothy 2:5). • *"The Lord is the true God; He is the living God and the everlasting King"* (Jeremiah 10:10). • *"In the beginning was the Word, and the Word was with God, and the Word was God"* (John 1:1), referring to Christ. • *"Jesus the Son of God"* (Hebrews 4:14). • *"Ananias, why has Satan filled your heart to lie to the Holy Spirit ... you have not lied to men but to God"* (Acts 5:3,4).

SALVATION	
People are saved by their own good life, where the good outweighs the bad. Believers can lose their salvation. God will not punish unbelievers eternally.	Salvation is by faith alone, by God's grace. It is eternally secure. Those not saved will face God's eternal punishment. • *"For by grace you have been saved through faith; and that not of yourselves, it is the gift of God"* (Ephesians 2:8). • *"I give eternal life to them, and they will never perish"* (John 10:28). • *"These will go away into eternal punishment, but the righteous into eternal life"* (Matthew 25:46). • *"He who believes in the Son has eternal life; but he who does not obey the Son will not see life, but the wrath of God abides on him"* (John 3:36).

THE WORK OF THE HOLY SPIRIT	
Miraculous gifts of the Spirit still apply today. All believers should pray to be baptized by the Holy Spirit as a second blessing, and speak in tongues (unknown languages).	Miraculous gifts (such as the ability to speak in unknown languages and to heal people) were given to some believers in the early days of the apostles to validate their new teaching, before the New Testament Scriptures were complete. Believers are baptized "in" (not "by") the Holy Spirit at the time of their salvation. Thereafter they are exhorted to be filled with the Spirit. Tongues were only used as a sign of the giving of the Holy Spirit in new circumstances (Acts 2:4;10:46;19:6). Otherwise, during the apostolic period, they were to be used very selectively, and only with an interpreter (1 Corinthians 14:5). • *"After it was at the first spoken through the Lord, it was confirmed to us by those who heard, God also testifying with them, both by signs and wonders and by various miracles and by gifts of the Holy Spirit according to His own will"* (Hebrews 2:3,4). • *"By one Spirit we were all baptized into one body"* (1 Corinthians 12:13). • *"Be filled with the Spirit"* (Ephesians 5:18). • *"All do not have gifts of healings, do they? All do not speak with tongues, do they?"* (1 Corinthians 12:30)

BAPTISM	
Baptism is necessary for salvation. Sprinkling is an acceptable alternative to immersion. Infants should be baptized (sprinkled, "christened"). Baptism is optional for a disciple. Baptism need not be into the name of the Father and of the Son and of the Holy Spirit.	Salvation is by faith alone. • *"For by grace you have been saved through faith; and that not of your-selves, it is the gift of God not as a result of works, so that no one may boast"* (Ephesians 2:8,9). • *"Therefore, having been justified by faith, we have peace with God through our Lord Jesus Christ"* (Romans 5:1). Baptism is a public testimony to our salvation. • *"So then, those who had received his word were baptized"* (Acts 2:41). Jesus was baptized, although He did not need salvation. • *"Jesus answering said to him, 'Permit it at this time; for in this way it is fit-ting for us to fulfill all righteousness.' Then he permitted Him. After being baptized, Jesus came up immediately from the water"* (Matthew 3:15,16). Baptism is by immersion in water. It symbolizes being identified with the burial and resurrection of Christ. • *"He ordered the chariot to stop; and they both went down into the water, Philip as well as the eunuch, and he baptized him. When they came up out of the water, the Spirit of the Lord snatched Philip away"* (Acts 8:38,39).

	• *"Do you not know that all of us who have been baptized into Christ Jesus have been baptized into His death? Therefore we have been buried with Him through baptism into death, so that as Christ was raised from the dead through the glory of the Father, so we too might walk in newness of life"* (Romans 6:3,4). Believers are commanded to be baptized; it requires a response of obedience. • *"He ordered them to be baptized in the name of Jesus Christ"* (Acts 10:48). The Lord instructed His apostles to baptize disciples into the name of the Father and of the Son and of the Holy Spirit. • *"Go therefore and make disciples of all the nations, baptizing them in* [Greek "eis": into] *the name of the Father and the Son and the Holy Spirit"* (Matthew 28:19).

CHURCH GATHERING	
Believers are free to worship wherever and however they choose. All believers are in the priesthood. Salvation is the only requirement for church membership and for keeping the Lord's Supper. Believers and unbelievers can worship together.	God has prescribed churches of God where baptized disciples should be added. • *"To the church of God which is at Corinth, to those who have been sanctified in Christ Jesus, saints by calling ... "* (1 Corinthians 1:2). • *"So then, those who had received his word were baptized; and that day there were added about three thousand souls"* (Acts 2:41).

God "calls" disciples into "the fellowship of His Son," a community of disciples committed to unitedly carrying out the Lord's commands as taught by His apostles.

- *"God is faithful, by whom you were called into the fellowship of His Son, Jesus Christ our Lord"* (1 Corinthians 1:9 NKJV).

This community constitutes the house of God, where those disciples who have been built into it can worship God as a holy priesthood. Unbelievers, unbaptized believers, and believers not added to a church of God do not have this privilege.

- *"So then you are no longer strangers and aliens, but you are fellow citizens with the saints, and are of God's household, having been built on the foundation of the apostles and prophets, Christ Jesus Himself being the corner stone, in whom the whole building, being fitted together, is growing into a holy temple in the Lord, in whom you also are being built together into a dwelling of God in the Spirit"* (Ephesians 2:19-22).

- *"You also, as living stones, are being built up as a spiritual house for a holy priesthood, to offer up spiritual sacrifices acceptable to God through Jesus Christ"* (1 Peter 2:5).

- *"John to the seven churches that are in Asia ... To Him who loves us and released us from our sins by His blood—and He has made us to be a kingdom, priests to His God and Father"* (Revelation 1:4-6).

LEADERSHIP	
Apostles should be appointed today. Since only apostles can appoint elders and there are not any apostles today, elders should not be appointed. Clergy should be appointed to carry out the service of the church. Women may undertake leadership roles. Each church can be independent of others.	Apostles of the Lord Jesus were men who had seen Him and received their teaching directly from Him, and so there can be no apostles today. • *"Am I not an apostle? Have I not seen Jesus our Lord?"* (1 Corinthians 9:1) • *"I received from the Lord that which I also delivered to you"* (1 Corinthians 11:23). The apostle Paul instructed Titus (not an apostle) to appoint elders. • *"For this reason I left you in Crete, that you would set in order what remains and appoint elders in every city as I directed you"* (Titus 1:5). Elders are "among" the saints. • *"I exhort the elders among you, as your fellow elder ... shepherd the flock of God among you"* (1 Peter 5:1,2). All the saints in a church of God should actively engage in its service. • *"When you assemble, each one has a psalm, has a teaching, has a revelation, has a tongue, has an interpretation. Let all things be done for edification"* (1 Corinthians 14:26). Women are not to exercise authority over men in the church. • *"I do not allow a woman to teach or exercise authority over a man, but to remain quiet"* (1 Timothy 2:12).

	Churches of God are to follow the same teaching, and support each other. Their elders should be united.
	• *"So I direct in all the churches"* (1 Corinthians 7:17).
	• *"When Paul and Barnabas had great dissension and debate with them, the brethren determined that Paul and Barnabas and some others of them should go up to Jerusalem to the apostles and elders concerning this issue"* (Acts 15:2).
	• *"While they were passing through the cities, they were delivering the decrees which had been decided upon by the apostles and elders who were in Jerusalem, for them to observe. So the churches were being strengthened in the faith, and were increasing in number daily"* (Acts 16:4,5).

C.

Comments on Selected Scriptures

Many New Testament Scriptures have been referred to throughout this book. Some of these are particularly relevant to establishing the spiritual position of disciples of the Lord Jesus in (a) the church the Body of Christ, (b) the house of God, and (c) churches of God. Following is a fuller commentary on these aspects of some of these passages, in their context.

Matthew 28:18–20

> *"And Jesus came up and spoke to them, saying, 'All authority has been given to Me in heaven and on earth. Go therefore and make disciples of all the nations, baptizing them in the name of the Father and the Son and the Holy Spirit, teaching them to observe all that I commanded you; and lo, I am with you always, even to the end of the age.'"*

This was one of the Lord's final acts on Earth before He ascended to heaven. In it He announced that God had given Him total authority, both in heavenly realms (1 Peter 3:22) and throughout the Earth. The apostle Peter preached that Jesus is Lord a few days later at Pentecost (Acts 2:36). When a person becomes a disciple, Jesus does not become their Lord; He is already Lord of all (Acts 10:36). The person is acknowledging the fact that He is their Lord and is willingly subjecting themselves to Him.

Jesus then gave them what is often referred to as the "Great Commission." The apostles were to go and make disciples of all nationalities. The gospel was to be worldwide (although it was restricted initially to the Jews). Making a disciple is more than telling people to believe in Jesus Christ for eternal life; it also involves bringing them to the point of submitting themselves to follow Him as Lord. They were to baptize and teach those disciples. In fact, the wording shows that the baptizing and teaching were an integral part of making them disciples—literally *"make disciples, baptizing and teaching them."* There is no support given in Scripture for the notion of believing for salvation but not also following as a disciple.

The baptism was to be "*into*" (Greek: *eis*) the name (singular) of the Father and the Son and the Holy Spirit. A person is baptized (immersed) "*by*" another disciple, "*in*" water, "*into*" that name (indicating the deity and authority of the Lord Jesus Christ). [28]

These words "*into the name of the Father and of the Son and of the Holy Spirit*" are not repeated in subsequent references to disciples' baptism in the book of Acts. However the fact that it is so explicit in this first mention by the Lord Himself, and carries such significance, shows that this is how it should be done today.

Acts 1:1–5

> "*The first account I composed, Theophilus, about all that Jesus began to do and teach, until the day when He was taken up to heaven, after He had by the Holy Spirit given orders to the apostles whom He had chosen. To these He also presented Himself alive after His suffering, by many convincing proofs, appearing to them over a period of forty days and speaking of the things concerning the kingdom of God. Gathering them together, He commanded them not to leave Jerusalem, but to wait for what the Father had promised, 'Which,' He said, 'you heard of from Me; for John baptized with water, but you will be baptized with the Holy Spirit not many days from now.'*"

This forty-day period that the Lord Jesus spent on Earth with His eleven apostles, between His resurrection and His ascension to heaven, was an intense time of learning for them. He was preparing them for the task of carrying on His work in His absence. He gave them commandments to keep, and He instructed them to teach them all to the new disciples who would believe through their word (Matthew 28:20; John 17:20). We are not told explicitly what He said, but we can deduce it clearly from what they did after He left.

The overall subject was the kingdom of God. The kingdom had been taken away from the nation of Israel, because of their disobedience (Matthew 21:43). He was now about to give it to them and to those joined with them, at Pentecost, as the "little flock" (Luke 12:32). After His departure, that is what they preached and taught—"the kingdom of God"—as the book of Acts describes throughout. It was how disciples were to live and serve together, keeping all that the Lord had commanded. At the end of the book of Acts the apostle Paul was in Rome still "*preaching the kingdom of God and teaching concerning the Lord Jesus Christ*" (Acts 28:31).

The power within them in carrying out this commission was to be the Holy Spirit, which God was about to pour out on them and others, beginning at

---

28 Correspondingly, our spiritual baptism at the time of our salvation is "*by*" Christ (John 1:33), "*in*" the Holy Spirit, "*into*" the Body of Christ (1 Corinthians 12:13).

Pentecost. They were not to begin this work until they received Him. This was not a work they could do on their own.

Acts 2:41–47

> *"So then, those who had received his word were baptized; and that day there were added about three thousand souls. They were continually devoting themselves to the apostles' teaching and to fellowship, to the breaking of bread and to prayer. Everyone kept feeling a sense of awe; and many wonders and signs were taking place through the apostles. And all those who had believed were together and had all things in common; and they began selling their property and possessions and were sharing them with all, as anyone might have need. Day by day continuing with one mind in the temple, and breaking bread from house to house, they were taking their meals together with gladness and sincerity of heart, praising God and having favor with all the people. And the Lord was adding to their number day by day those who were being saved."*

The hundred and twenty or so disciples had been waiting in Jerusalem for the Holy Spirit to come (Acts 1:15), as the Lord Jesus had promised them. Jerusalem was the place where He had so recently been crucified, and where His grave was, which was now empty. It was where the great temple was, which was being replaced as where God would be worshipped by His people. They were *"all together in one place"* (verse 1), called to be there by the Lord Himself, for one purpose. In effect, they were a church, although that word is not used. That is what a church is, a collection of people called out by God from wherever they were to be together for Him. However, they were about to become "the church of God in Jerusalem" with the arrival of the Holy Spirit.

The pouring out of the Spirit gave Peter his opportunity (and also the ability) to preach the gospel to the devout Jews who came to investigate. About three thousand of them responded to His preaching—they *"gladly received"* (NKJV) his word. They were all baptized and added to those who were already together. The formula of Matthew 28:19,20 was being carried out. The result was that on that day two divine things came into existence—the church the Body of Christ, that the Lord had spoken about in Matthew 16:18, and the church of God in Jerusalem. Those people became part of both of them, which is of course the ideal. However, that situation did not last, because being in a church of God requires on-going adherence to the Lord's teaching, while being in the Body does not.

The three things that are mentioned in verse 41 happened to each of them as individuals, and only need to happen once for each person—salvation, water baptism, and addition to a church of God. But they need to happen in that sequence.

And then verse 42 describes four things that the church was *"devoting themselves to"* (or *"continuing steadfastly in"* NKJV), that happened continually and were done collectively. Again the sequence is important. They continued in "the apostles teaching"—that is, they were taught and were obedient to what the Lord Jesus had taught the apostles during the forty days, as referred to in Acts 1:1–5. They also continued in the fellowship of the apostles and others; they were a community. They did not stay together and then decide what the teaching would be; they became in effect a partnership based on their common adherence to the full teaching. The teaching came first. That community was described later by the apostle Paul as *"the fellowship of His Son, Jesus Christ our Lord"* (1 Corinthians 1:9). Then it says that they continued in "the breaking of bread" (the remembrance of the Lord Jesus with the bread and wine, as He had commanded in Luke 22:19), and in "the prayers" (the gatherings for collective prayer, such as is recorded in Acts 12:5). These four things were vitally important and definitely worth devoting themselves to.

As noted in Appendix A, all four of these activities include the definite article. "The apostles' teaching" was a single body of doctrine. "The fellowship" was a single defined community. "The breaking of bread" was a regular defined service, distinct from "breaking bread" as in verse 46 (which refers to taking meals together). "The prayers" was a regular defined gathering for prayer by the church, distinct from praying individually or in informal groups. These seven steps in verses 41 and 42, in their proper order, set a pattern for us to follow today.

Acts 14:21–23

> *"After they had preached the gospel to that city and had made many disciples, they returned to Lystra and to Iconium and to Antioch, strengthening the souls of the disciples, encouraging them to continue in the faith, and saying, 'Through many tribulations we must enter the kingdom of God.' When they had appointed elders for them in every church, having prayed with fasting, they commended them to the Lord in whom they had believed."*

In his missionary journeys, the apostle Paul not only covered new territory, he often re-visited existing churches to strengthen them. Discipleship is an on-going matter and it requires continual support and building up. This is why he returned at this particular time to the three churches in these towns in the southern part of Asia Minor. In these verses we see the link that exists between: (a) "the faith" (the commands of the Lord; the apostles' teaching); (b) "the kingdom of God," the community where that teaching was practiced; (c) the "church" in each of those places, consisting of gatherings of disciples there; and (d) "elders," who had the God-given responsibility to care for those churches (1 Timothy 3:5).

Romans 6:17

"But thanks be to God that though you were slaves of sin, you became obedient from the heart to that form of teaching to which you were committed."

In Jude verse 3 we are told that the faith (the Lord's teaching for His disciples today) had been fully delivered to the saints. In this Scripture the reverse picture is given. Paul describes the saints as having been delivered to the doctrine. He describes it as a form, a mould or pattern, that they were being poured into. It would shape their lives and their service. Not only was the teaching delivered to them to keep, they were also delivered to it and must conform to it.

1 Corinthians 1:1,2,9

"Paul, called as an apostle of Jesus Christ by the will of God, and Sosthenes our brother, to the church of God which is at Corinth, to those who have been sanctified in Christ Jesus, saints by calling, with all who in every place call on the name of our Lord Jesus Christ, their Lord and ours: ... God is faithful, through whom you were called into fellowship with His Son, Jesus Christ our Lord."

In these three verses at the start of his first letter to the church at Corinth, the apostle Paul used the word "call" four times, with various meanings. (Variants of the word are used in the original Greek text.)

Firstly, he told those in the church that God had called him to be an apostle; that was his own unique calling to his life-work. Secondly, he told them that God had called them (summoned them, appointed them) to be "saints" (holy ones, set apart for God). This applied equally to all of them. Thirdly, he linked them with others in various places who "call on" the name of the Lord. This is a general term used quite widely in the Bible to refer to worshipping, praying, and responding to the Lord. It is used to refer to the church in Jerusalem when Paul himself was persecuting them (Acts 9:14). Finally he told them that God had called them into "the fellowship" of His Son, the community of those who were gathered in the same way as they were, in churches of God.

It was clear that those in the church were not just there by their own choice. They had responded to the call (summons) of God through the proclamation of His Word. They had been called into that local church, but also into the wider community. The definite article is present before the word "fellowship" in verse 9. It was a defined fellowship (partnership, community) belonging to the Lord Jesus, such as was referred to in Acts 2:42. It is not identical to fellowship "with" God as described in 1 John 1:3, although it certainly includes that.

1 Corinthians 3:9–17

"For we are God's fellow workers; you are God's field, God's building. According to the grace of God which was given to me, like a wise master builder I laid a foundation, and another is building on it. But each man must be careful how he builds on it. For no man can lay a foundation other than the one which is laid, which is Jesus Christ. Now if any man builds on the foundation with gold, silver, precious stones, wood, hay, straw, each man's work will become evident; for the day will show it because it is to be revealed with fire, and the fire itself will test the quality of each man's work. If any man's work which he has built on it remains, he will receive a reward. If any man's work is burned up, he will suffer loss; but he himself will be saved, yet so as through fire. Do you not know that you are a temple of God and that the Spirit of God dwells in you? If any man destroys the temple of God, God will destroy him, for the temple of God is holy, and that is what you are."

Here the apostle Paul is describing how the church of God in Corinth came into existence (as recorded in Acts 18:1–11). His primary role as an apostle there, as everywhere else, was to lay the foundation teaching about Christ. This was the apostles' teaching and it had to correspond entirely to the heavenly reality of Christ's position in heaven as the foundation stone of the spiritual house of God (1 Peter 2:6). Once the foundational teaching was established, it never needed to be amended or added to, but others in the church were to build on that by putting it into practice in their service for God. He warned them all that their works would be evaluated one day, and those would prove to have been positive ("gold, silver, or precious stones"), or worthless ("wood, hay, stubble"). The works may even be destructive (verse 17), for which there would be judgment. In verse 9 he described the church in Corinth as a building—not a physical building, of course, but what God was building in that city. It is a metaphor he also used later in Ephesians 2:21.

Then to the church he said, *"Do you not know that you are the temple of God?"* (verse 16). The definite article is not in the original text; literally it reads, *"You are temple of God."* The expression "temple of God" is another term for the house of God. The church of God in Corinth was not the whole house, of course, but they were part of it and they were expected to reflect its character of holiness.

1 Corinthians 11:18–26

"For, in the first place, when you come together as a church, I hear that divisions exist among you; and in part I believe it. For there must also be factions among you, so that those who are approved may become evident among you. Therefore when you meet together, it is not to eat the Lord's Supper, for in your eating each one takes his own supper first; and one is hungry and another is drunk. What! Do you not have houses in which to eat and drink? Or do you despise the church of God and shame those who have nothing? What shall I say to you? Shall I praise you? In this I will not praise you.

For I received from the Lord that which I also delivered to you, that the Lord Jesus in the night in which He was betrayed took bread; and when He had given thanks, He broke it and said, 'This is My body, which is for you; do this in remembrance of Me.' In the same way He took the cup also after supper, saying, 'This cup is the new covenant in My blood; do this, as often as you drink it, in remembrance of Me.' For as often as you eat this bread and drink the cup, you proclaim the Lord's death until He comes."

Paul is here correcting disorder in how the church was keeping the remembrance of the Lord Jesus, the Lord's Supper. It appears that they were treating it as a social event and, with the cliques that existed among them (1:10,11), they were acting very independently of one another and without proper regard for what the occasion meant. It was so serious that some of their number were sick and some had died, as a result of the Lord's judgment on them. Paul indicates that he obtained this teaching about the Lord's Supper directly from the Lord Jesus Himself (rather than from one of the other apostles who had been there in person on the night that the Lord instituted it). Paul makes it clear that the saints were to gather as a church for this remembrance, and not just as individuals. Their unity of heart and practice was vital. By acting as they had been doing, they had despised God's church, treating of little value something that was extremely precious to Him. It may only have been the actions of some of them, but they were a unit and it reflected on them all.

2 Corinthians 6:14–18

"Do not be bound together with unbelievers; for what partnership have righteousness and lawlessness, or what fellowship has light with darkness? Or what harmony has Christ with Belial, or what has a believer in common with an unbeliever? Or what agreement has the temple of God with idols? For we are the temple of the living God; just as God said, 'I will dwell in them and walk

among them; and I will be their God, and they shall be My people. Therefore, come out from their midst and be separate,' says the Lord. 'And do not touch what is unclean; and I will welcome you. And I will be a father to you, and you shall be sons and daughters to Me,' says the Lord Almighty."

Here, in his second letter to the church at Corinth, Paul was correcting the problem of their lack of separation from people who did not believe and practice God's truth. He told them that they could not keep their identity as God's people unless they came out from things that were opposed to it. There is no room for mixing truth with error, righteousness with unrighteousness, and the house of God with idolatry. They were being defiled by joining with what was not of God, and they needed to be cleansed of it. Because he was addressing them as a church of God (2 Corinthians 1:1), he shows that there is a clear link between it and the temple of God and the people of God (verse 16). If they would respond positively to this warning, he states, they would enjoy the presence of God in them [29] collectively as His own people, and He would treat them as His "sons and daughters" living with Him in His house. This was something beyond their relationship with Christ in the church which is His Body, in which there are no gender distinctions of sons and daughters (Galatians 3:28). The expression *"walk among them"* is reminiscent of the vision that John saw later of the Lord Jesus walking among the seven churches (Revelation 2:1).

Ephesians 2:19–22

"So then you are no longer strangers and aliens, but you are fellow citizens with the saints, and are of God's household, having been built on the foundation of the apostles and prophets, Christ Jesus Himself being the corner stone, in whom the whole building, being fitted together, is growing into a holy temple in the Lord, in whom you also are being built together into a dwelling of God in the Spirit."

In this chapter, the apostle Paul describes what had happened to the Gentile (non-Jewish) saints in the church in Ephesus. He starts the chapter by describing them before their salvation, when they had been *"dead in your trespasses and sins,"* and finishes the chapter with them being *"a dwelling of God in the Spirit."* What a transformation! In these final four verses, He uses the following expressions to describe them:

---

29 The quotation is from Leviticus 26:11,12 where it states: *"I will make my dwelling among you..."*. In 2 Corinthians 6:16 it has been changed by the Holy Spirit to: *"I will dwell in* [Greek: 'en'] *them..."*.

- *"Fellow citizens with the saints"*—they had equal status with Jewish disciples, something they had never enjoyed in Old Testament times.

- *"Of God's household"*—they were part of the spiritual house, living stones built into it.

- *"Having been built on the foundation of the apostles and prophets, Christ Jesus Himself being the corner stone*—just as in Corinth, Paul had laid the foundation teaching of the Lord in Ephesus (as the other apostles and New Testament prophets were also doing elsewhere). That foundation teaching corresponded to what God had done in establishing Christ as the foundation of the spiritual house in heaven. Adhering to this teaching was the basis on which those saints had become part of that house.

- *"In whom the whole* [every] *building, being fitted together, is growing into a holy temple in the Lord"*—the Greek word translated "whole," *"pas,"* is used numerous times in the New Testament and always in the plural, usually translated as *"every."* This does not refer to a single building, but to several. This translation has led some people to assume that Paul was referring here to the church the Body of Christ, which is not the case. What Paul was describing is that each church of God, as it is properly linked with the others, constitutes the house (temple) of God. The individual disciples as living stones (1 Peter 2:5) were being built together town by town, in churches of God, and together they formed God's house on Earth.

- *"In whom you also are being built together into a dwelling of God in the Spirit"*—he then tells the church in Ephesus that they too were part of that process. There had to be unity of teaching and practice within each church (*"built together,"* verse 22), and also among all the churches (*"fitted together,"* verse 21). God could then dwell among them on Earth (the Greek word means a "down-dwelling place") collectively in the person of the Holy Spirit (in addition to Him residing individually in their bodies).

Ephesians 4:7–16

"But to each one of us grace was given according to the measure of Christ's gift. Therefore it says, 'When He ascended on high, He led captive a host of captives, and He gave gifts to men.' (Now this expression, 'He ascended,' what does it mean except that He also had descended into the lower parts of the earth? He who descended is Himself also He who ascended far above all the

heavens, so that He might fill all things.) And He gave some as apostles, and some as prophets, and some as evangelists, and some as pastors and teachers, for the equipping of the saints for the work of service, to the building up of the body of Christ; until we all attain to the unity of the faith, and of the knowledge of the Son of God, to a mature man, to the measure of the stature which belongs to the fullness of Christ. As a result, we are no longer to be children, tossed here and there by waves and carried about by every wind of doctrine, by the trickery of men, by craftiness in deceitful scheming; but speaking the truth in love, we are to grow up in all aspects into Him who is the head, even Christ, from whom the whole body, being fitted and held together by what every joint supplies, according to the proper working of each individual part, causes the growth of the body for the building up of itself in love."

In this Scripture Paul is describing the process by which living members of the Body of Christ, which he had referred to in chapter 1 as *"the fullness of Him who fills all in all,"* are built up. Designated men were initially given as gifts to equip the saints for their service, which was intended to bring believers to *"the unity of the faith"* (that is, united adherence to all the teaching of the Lord) and *"of the knowledge of the Son of God"* (that is, united relationship with Christ in all His present capacities on their behalf). In this way all believers would come to experience Christ, not only as their Saviour, but also as their Lord in their obedience, as their Shepherd for receiving direction and care, as their High Priest in their collective worship and service, as their Advocate when they sin, as their Intercessor when they pray, and more. This goal represents full maturity of believers, which would be arrived at when they were fully developed and fully integrated in mutual support and co-ordinated service according to the commands of the Lord. The full measure of that is the stature of Christ Himself. Therefore, becoming a member of the Body of Christ is not an end in itself, but the beginning of a process designed to bring all members together to full expression of the person of Christ. We have a long way to go.

1 Timothy 3:14,15

"I am writing these things to you, hoping to come to you before long; but in case I am delayed, I write so that you will know how one ought to conduct himself in the household of God, which is the church of the living God, the pillar and support of the truth."

These verses come at the end of the lists of qualities that Paul was giving Timothy for him to look for in men who should be appointed as overseers and deacons in the churches. These churches together constituted the house (sometimes translated *"household"*) of God, and these leadership roles were established by the Lord to govern behaviour in that house. The house is described here as *"the church of the living God."* It is the entire congregation of those called out from the world to be gathered together in local churches, to stand as a testimony to the truth of God. Being in the Body of Christ is based on our confession of Jesus Christ as *"the Son of the living God"* (Matthew 16:16–18), while being gathered together in service and testimony according to the call of God places us in *"the church of the living God."*

Hebrews 3:1–6

> *"Therefore, holy brethren, partakers of a heavenly calling, consider Jesus, the Apostle and High Priest of our confession; He was faithful to Him who appointed Him, as Moses also was in all His house. For He has been counted worthy of more glory than Moses, by just so much as the builder of the house has more honor than the house. For every house is built by someone, but the builder of all things is God. Now Moses was faithful in all His house as a servant, for a testimony of those things which were to be spoken later; but Christ was faithful as a Son over His house—whose house we are, if we hold fast our confidence and the boast of our hope firm until the end."*

Christ is presented in this passage both as the apostle and high priest of our confession. Our confession is what we profess about the truth of God, as taught by Christ. As the apostle, Christ came out from God to confess this truth to mankind. As the priest He has gone back into God's presence to confess it to God on behalf of those who hold it. What is highlighted here is His faithfulness in doing that. A comparison is made to Moses' faithfulness in making the tabernacle exactly as he was told to, because of what it represented, but his status was only that of a servant. Christ's status is that of the son who has all authority over the house of God.

God is building His spiritual house today as disciples are being built into it as "living stones" (1 Peter 2:5). They participate in that as long as they hold fast to their belief in their "hope." That is not referring to the hope of their future salvation, the hope of Christ coming from heaven for them. Rather, it is the reality of Christ being now in heaven which provides the present opportunity of them going in together to God in worship. It is defined in chapter 6:19 (*"a hope both sure and steadfast and one which enters within the veil"*) and in 7:19 (*"a better hope, through which we draw near to God"*). Thus, being included in the house of God is a conditional matter and quite distinct, for example, from being in the church the

Body of Christ. The faithfulness of both Christ and Moses are highlighted here to stress the need for our faithfulness in doing this.

Hebrews 10:19–25; 12:18–24,28; 13:15

> *"Therefore, brethren, since we have confidence to enter the holy place by the blood of Jesus, by a new and living way which He inaugurated for us through the veil, that is, His flesh, and since we have a great priest over the house of God, let us draw near with a sincere heart in full assurance of faith, having our hearts sprinkled clean from an evil conscience and our bodies washed with pure water. Let us hold fast the confession of our hope without wavering, for He who promised is faithful; and let us consider how to stimulate one another to love and good deeds, not forsaking our own assembling together, as is the habit of some, but encouraging one another; and all the more as you see the day drawing near....*
>
> *For you have not come to a mountain that can be touched and to a blazing fire, and to darkness and gloom and whirlwind, and to the blast of a trumpet and the sound of words which sound was such that those who heard begged that no further word be spoken to them. For they could not bear the command, 'If even a beast touches the mountain, it will be stoned.' And so terrible was the sight, that Moses said, 'I am full of fear and trembling.' But you have come to Mount Zion and to the city of the living God, the heavenly Jerusalem, and to myriads of angels, to the general assembly and church of the firstborn who are enrolled in heaven, and to God, the Judge of all, and to the spirits of the righteous made perfect, and to Jesus, the mediator of a new covenant, and to the sprinkled blood, which speaks better than the blood of Abel....*
>
> *Therefore, since we receive a kingdom which cannot be shaken, let us show gratitude, by which we may offer to God an acceptable service with reverence and awe....*
>
> *Through Him then, let us continually offer up a sacrifice of praise to God, that is, the fruit of lips that give thanks to His name."*

These Scriptures in Hebrews represent the summit of the epistle. From chapter 1 it climbs through magnificent truths and inescapable reasoning to this climax— *"therefore ... let us draw near."* This is how we give effect to our holding fast the confession of our hope. We approach God in our spirits, fully assured by faith that we are drawing near in heaven itself, based on the person of Jesus Christ (*"the veil, that is, His flesh"*) and the blood, which He shed and which has been applied to deal for ever with our sins. Unlike the Old Testament worshippers, our hearts have (symbolically) had the blood of Christ applied to them to cleanse our consciences from sin (Hebrews 9:14), and we have been cleansed (symbolically) by *"the washing of water with the word"* (Ephesians 5:26) from all defilement.

In addition, our relationships with each other must be right because this service is collective. We are told to not stop assembling. We gather on Earth to give our spiritual sacrifices audibly (*"the fruit of lips"*), whereby we confess God's name to Him *"so that with one accord you may with one voice glorify the God and Father of our Lord Jesus Christ"* (Romans 15:6). The words in Hebrews 12:28, *"let us show gratitude,"* are translated in the NKJV as *"let us have grace,"* showing that our response to receiving the grace of God in our hearts is to express our appreciation to Him. We do this in an attitude of complete reverence.

Our worship takes place *"in spirit and in truth"* (John 4:24) in heaven, not on Earth, in the place to which we have come—the heavenly city of Jerusalem on the heavenly Mount Zion. Countless worshipping angels are there, as are the souls of believers from the Old and New Testaments who have passed on. God the Father is there on His throne to receive the worship, and Jesus is there as a man, as our mediator. He has made our access to the holy place and our worship possible, on the basis of His shed blood, which satisfies all God's demands. In contrast, Abel's blood called out to God for revenge (Genesis 4:10); but Christ's blood has brought peace (Colossians 1:20). Just as blood was sprinkled in front of and on the mercy seat in the Old Testament sanctuary (Leviticus 16:14), so it is seen here (symbolically) as being in the sanctuary in heaven for us. This collective worship in God's sanctuary in heaven is the highest service possible for created beings today.

1 Peter 2:1–10

"Therefore, putting aside all malice and all deceit and hypocrisy and envy and all slander, like newborn babies, long for the pure milk of the word, so that by it you may grow in respect to salvation, if you have tasted the kindness of the Lord. And coming to Him as to a living stone which has been rejected by men, but is choice and precious in the sight of God, you also, as living stones, are being built up as a spiritual house for a holy priesthood, to offer up spiritual sacrifices acceptable to God through Jesus Christ. For this is contained in Scripture: 'Behold, I lay in Zion a choice stone, a precious corner stone, and he who believes in Him will not be disappointed.' This precious value, then, is for you who believe; but for those who disbelieve, 'The stone which the builders rejected, this became the very corner stone,' and, 'a stone of stumbling and a rock of offense'; for they stumble because they are disobedient to the word, and to this doom they were also appointed. But you are a chosen race, a royal

priesthood, a holy nation, a people for God's own possession, so that you may proclaim the excellencies of Him who has called you out of darkness into His marvelous light; for you once were not a people, but now you are the people of God; you had not received mercy, but now you have received mercy."

The disciples that Peter was writing to had been born again (1 Peter 1:21,23) and then been built in, as "*living stones,*" to God's spiritual house. This was by means of them coming to Christ as their Lord, not initially for salvation, but continually (as the tense of the verb shows) in obedience to Him. As they engaged in their spiritual service together, the house was continually being built up. Its function was to be a "holy priesthood"—that is, to offer service wholly to God, as one united entity. The job of a high priest is to be an intermediary, to represent the people to God. Christ is our high priest. Through Him, we have access as a priesthood. All believers have a birthright to be priests, but they must be built into the house to function together as the priesthood, because priestly service is collective service.

It is the work of priests to bring sacrifices to God (Hebrews 9:6); they are offered for the people through the high priest (Hebrews 5:1; 13:11). As the holy priesthood, we offer spiritual sacrifices that Christ makes perfect and offers to God on our behalf.

The spiritual house has its foundation in heaven in the exalted Christ, who was rejected by men on Earth but glorified by His Father upon His return. This priesthood is also described as being "royal"—literally "a kingdom of priests" (see also Revelation 1:6), just as Israel had been described under the old covenant (Exodus 19:6). It is also described as "a holy nation" and "a people for God's own possession," showing the unity and identity of those who gather in obedience to Him. Its purpose is to testify to the excellencies of God, who has called them out of spiritual darkness to reveal to them the light of His truth. We see in this passage the linkage between the house of God, the kingdom of God, and the people of God. It was written to people who had been baptized (3:21) and were under the rule of elders (5:1–3), which identifies them as being in churches of God.

Jude verse 3

"Beloved, while I was making every effort to write you about our common salvation, I felt the necessity to write to you appealing that you contend earnestly for the faith which was once for all handed down to the saints."

Jude distinguishes here between the salvation that all believers have in common and "the faith." The faith is the complete body of teaching to be adhered to (see also Appendix B). It includes our common salvation, but also much more. We do not have to contend for our salvation, but we do have to contend for the faith. For example, the apostle Paul said towards the end of his life, "*I have kept the faith*" (2 Timothy 4:7). This body of teaching was originally commanded by the Lord Jesus to His apostles before His ascension to heaven (Acts 1:2). In Matthew 28:18–20, He instructed them to teach the newly baptized disciples "*all that I commanded you.*" It was a complete teaching, which was then taught by the apostles to those who believed, becoming known as "*the apostles' teaching*" (Acts 2:42). It was later that it became known as "the faith" (Acts 6:7; 14:22; etc.). By the time Jude wrote this epistle, the faith had been completely passed on to the saints. It was the foundational teaching of the churches. It had been the task of the apostles to put it in place, and it was not to be added to or changed. It is just as relevant and complete today as it was then. We have the great advantage of having it documented for us in the New Testament Scriptures.

Revelation 1:4–6

"John to the seven churches that are in Asia: Grace to you and peace, from Him who is and who was and who is to come, and from the seven Spirits who are before His throne, and from Jesus Christ, the faithful witness, the firstborn of the dead, and the ruler of the kings of the earth. To Him who loves us and released us from our sins by His blood—and He has made us to be a kingdom, priests to His God and Father—to Him be the glory and the dominion forever and ever. Amen."

The apostle John was writing to the seven churches of God that were in Asia Minor. He included, in chapters 2 and 3, specific messages that he was given by the Lord Jesus to each of them. Those churches are described as "lampstands" in verse 20. It was those in the churches that had been made "*a kingdom, priests to His God and Father.*" The expression "*kingdom, priests*" is equivalent to the expression "*royal priesthood*" in 1 Peter 2:9 (and corresponds to "*kingdom of priests*" in Exodus 19:6, where it was part of the promise to Israel under the old covenant). It is referring to the kingdom of God, in which Christ is now both king and high priest. The Lord is described here as being among His churches, walking among them (2:1), the same expression that is used in 2 Corinthians 6:16 regarding the temple and people of God. He has authority over these churches. The kingdom, the priesthood, and the house were closely linked under the old covenant, just as they are under the new covenant today.

Epilogue

Why I Wrote This Book

It has been on my heart for a long, long time to try to write a book like this. Not that I necessarily thought that I was the right person to do it, but it needed doing and the conviction just would not go away.

Through no credit to me, God has squarely laid His hand on my life, and He has brought me to the point, at sixty-four years of age, where His things are by far the most important in my life, and what I spend most of my time on. This is not to suggest that I neglect other vital areas of my life, especially my family, but I see these as being within the greater context of the Lord's will for my life. Each one of my family is a wonderful gift from God.

I am often frustrated at my failures and ineffectiveness in the Lord's service, but my passion for it is stronger than ever. I am so grateful that He has brought me to a place in my life where what the world has on offer—status, recognition and financial rewards, some of which I have known in my professional career—have fallen into their proper place in the overall scheme of things.

I was brought up in a very godly Christian home and, the older I get, the more profoundly grateful I become for the values, scriptural teaching, and example that I learned from both my parents. I was saved (personally brought to know the Lord) at the very early age of five—and yet there is no doubt in my mind that it was my real conversion. I was baptized and added to the church of God in Glasgow, Scotland, at the age of eight, simply because I knew it was what I should do to be a disciple of the Lord Jesus. At age eleven, our family emigrated to Canada and we transferred to the church of God in Hamilton, Ontario. Three years later we moved to the big city of Toronto, where I have lived in one place or another ever since. We transferred at that time to the church of God in Toronto.

Around age twenty, while I was at university, I went through my first spiritual crisis. I began to have serious doubts about the very existence of God. I never spoke to anyone else about it at the time, although they may have suspected. It was my age of enlightenment, where I was sorting out which of the beliefs that I had inherited were truly my own. The process lasted for several months and it was a very uncomfortable time. But God revealed Himself to me in an unmistakable way.

In 1967, my wife Sandra and I were married, and over the years our children—Adele, Jennifer, and Andrew—were born. I am deeply grateful to God that each of them for themselves has made a deep and lasting commitment to the Lord Jesus, and are serving Him. My marriage to Sandra of forty years has been a hugely beneficial and stabilizing force in my life. She is a very godly, gifted, and caring woman.

Throughout my growing-up years, I learned more and more from the Bible, including the teaching of the churches of God that I was part of. I became convinced of it, which is not surprising, given my environment that reinforced it, and I even began teaching it to other young people. Teaching the Scriptures to young people and young adults has always been my passion. Watching the light go on in their eyes as they discover the reality of God in their lives has always been a big motivator for me.

However, in the early 1970s, my second major spiritual crisis took place. There were several men in our church, of varying ages older than me, whom I looked up to. They seemed far more knowledgeable and experienced than I was, and I tended to take what they said without question. But a few of them began to leave the church. I know now that it was largely due to a variety of personal reasons, but I was drawn into some in-depth scriptural discussions about doctrine with two of them. They began to question many of the fundamental teachings of the church, which I had always accepted. I found myself trying to defend these teachings. I was de-stabilized by the whole exercise. This inner turmoil prompted me eventually to begin an in-depth study of these things from the Scriptures, without reference to secondary sources or reliance on existing literature. Those were the days before home computers and electronic concordances, and I generated reams and reams of paper in the course of my study. What began to emerge was a pattern of teaching that seemed eventually to all fit together. When I asked those who were disputing these things for their alternate explanation of how these Scriptures related to one other, they never gave me one. It seemed that they had a lot more questions than answers.

I was nearing the end of my research when, in a single week, two personal letters arrived. One was from an older brother in the Lord three thousand miles to the west, in British Columbia. The other was from my uncle, three thousand miles to the east, in Great Britain. They had both heard of the unrest in our church and were concerned for me as a young man. The letters were both hugely encouraging, and they came at a strategic time for me. The one from my uncle included a particular offer of assistance, which I decided to take up. I wrote a rather terse letter listing ten key questions, which got to the heart of the dispute, and I asked for something more than the traditional answers to these. Within just a few days a reply arrived, several pages thick, containing a detailed scriptural response to each of my questions. As I read them over and over, I realized that I had been given real meat! It helped me immeasurably. (As you might expect, I still have the letter.)

As the months went by, the Lord again confirmed His Word to me. The other men eventually left the church and went various places. Even though I may not have been able to convince them, I had become convinced myself, and that was what mattered to me. It had taken me to a completely new level, and it bred in me a deep desire that more Christians should see what I had been shown—the marvellous truth in Scripture of the house of God and the churches of God. One by-product of that exercise was a self-study course that I developed, called *Where is God's House Today?* I am convinced that had this teaching not been so seriously challenged in my mind, I would never have come to the depth of understanding and conviction that I did about it, and for that I thank God.

On two subsequent occasions in the years since then I have felt led to re-examine these truths in detail, taking a different starting point each time. On both occasions, I found affirmation in the truth of the teaching, and in both cases my understanding and appreciation of it broadened and deepened. For that reason, I hope it happens again. A by-product of the first of these re-examinations was the teaching video and booklet *Uncovering the Pattern,* which was in use for several years.

While this topic is not by any means the only focus of my on-going teaching ministry to young people and adults, I welcome every opportunity to convey it to other disciples who are willing to consider it. Without a doubt, it is a revelation from God.

The unrest and division that I see among Christians has troubled me a great deal over the years—so much moving about from church to church, without any apparent deep conviction of where they ought to gather; so much disunity among members of the Body of Christ, which can't be solved by "papering over" differences of understanding. I also see it when people from time to time leave the churches of God with which I am associated. In talking with them, all too often they don't seem to realize what they are leaving, and that is sad. There is so much fragmentation among groups of believers today, so many denominations, so many different teachings. We are all members of the Body of Christ—we share that spiritual oneness—but the Lord Himself longed that the oneness might be shown in how we live our lives for Him. He prayed for that unity on His last night before Calvary. And yet these days our culture so celebrates individuality and diversity that we can lose sight of the goal of unity of purpose and unity of service in carrying out all that the Lord has left us to do for Him. As a colleague of mine once said, "We are all accountable for what we do with the apostles' teaching." Even though it is now the twenty-first century, it *is* relevant; it *is* applicable; it *is* vitally important. But it is not well known, and that is a problem.

My on-going study over the years caused me to try to understand what brought about the differences of view and practice that so pervade the Christian world today. This led me into studying Christian history from secular writings, which continue the story after the New Testament leaves off towards the end of the first century. I have found this a fascinating study, full of personal stories of peoples' lives. I have come to be full of admiration for so many of them—for example, for the early martyrs like Polycarp and Perpetua who, despite their limited under-standing, were so faithful to their Lord, even to the point of death. And to the Reformers, such as Wycliffe, Luther, Zwingli, Hus and Tyndale, to whom we owe so much. And then to godly men like the Wesley brothers and John Knox, as God was gradually revealing His truth, and more and more of it was being recov-ered. And then to the young men who founded the "Brethren," such as Darby and Mueller and Newton, who broke away from the established churches so that they could put into practice what they saw in Scripture. And to men like Banks and Boswell who, together with others, rediscovered the profound truth of the churches of God and the house of God and would not let it go. What a legacy I had.

It helped me to see why practices such as infant baptism came in and why it is held so tenaciously by some people; about the emergence of a clergy distinct from a congregation that had become passive; about the insistence on the independ-ence of assemblies; about differences in leadership structures; about differences of understanding regarding certain gifts of the Spirit; and so on, and so on. These all emerged over the centuries, and in many cases they were honest differences of understanding about Scripture. The result is that the Christian world now is a far cry from its early years—there is an almost unlimited variety of beliefs, prac-tices, and churches. And traditions die hard. It is often difficult for any of us to distinguish between the clear teaching of Scripture and a practice that has been entrenched in our minds for a long time. And so the Body of Christ does not yet have "the unity of the faith" that the Lord intends for it. Is there one right church? Does it exist today? Does it even matter? These questions bothered me, but what could I do about it?

At some point along this journey the idea of this book was born. I do not actu-ally remember when it was. The impetus to get down to the effort of writing it has come and gone over the years, but overall the desire has strengthened rather than weakened. Those (very) few people that I mentioned it to from time to time encouraged me to do it.

As I peruse Christian bookstores, read my share of books by Christian authors, and listen to teachers and preachers on television and on CDs, there is much that I enjoy and benefit from. But it surprises me that there is such a void about the aspect of the collective service of God, which is so central in God's Word. Perhaps positional teaching is out of fashion just now, or perhaps it is the way it sometimes tends to be presented, but so much today seems to be only about personal Christian living. This aspect is absolutely necessary, of course, but it is not sufficient. It should lead us to what God is working towards—unity in collective service, things that we ought to be doing together. I have become convinced that all God's purposes are eventually collective, and I fall short if I see only the individual aspects. But we live in an individualistic age. For example, most of the Christian songs that are written today seem to be written from that point of view.

In 1988, while at the height of my professional career and family responsibilities, I was diagnosed with leukemia and told there was no cure. That was to change my life in a profound way over the ten years that I had it. After being told in 1991 that I had about two years to live, and after having had numerous rounds of very heavy chemotherapy (many of which were experimental), I received a bone marrow transplant in 1997 from my younger sister Hilary, after being told by the doctors that it would never happen. However, a year later, with the statistics against me, I was declared in complete remission. Looking back over it all, there was a succession of miraculous occurrences that showed it was all in God's hands. God has also blessed me with good health since then. (I tell the story of my ten years with leukemia in my book *I Want to Live,* which is available on request. Contact information is provided on page 145.) It became increasingly apparent to me over this whole time that God had unfinished business with me, and I have become increasingly convinced that a part of that business is for me to share this glorious truth that He has showed to me and others. It is in this spirit that I send this book forth, to see what God intends to do with it.

I am well aware that what is written here is not universally, or even generally, held among Christians. If it were, I probably would never have felt the need to write it. For this reason, I fully expect a wide variety of reactions to it. That is not within my control—I am quite content to leave the outcome with God. But I would be remiss if I did not at least try to communicate it to others, and that is what impels me. And so, as Pontius Pilate once said, "What I have written, I have written." I want very much, however, to engage in any constructive dialogue over the Scriptures with any honest seeker after God, and I would welcome such enquiries. Contact information is given on page 145.

If you have read this far in this personal epilogue, I thank you. I hope that you have or will read this book carefully, referring to the Scriptures noted, asking the

Lord to show you what He wants you to draw from it. It is the work of the Spirit of God to lead us into all the truth of Christ. When He does so, it is then up to us to do it.

Keith Dorricott
November 2007

978-0-595-43392-6
0-595-43392-8

Printed in the United States
97834LV00004B/1-153/A